CAMBRIDGE LIBRARY COLLECTION

Books of enduring scholarly value

Printing and Publishing History

The interface between authors and their readers is a fascinating subject in its own right, revealing a great deal about social attitudes, technological progress, aesthetic values, fashionable interests, political positions, economic constraints, and individual personalities. This part of the Cambridge Library Collection reissues classic studies in the area of printing and publishing history that shed light on developments in typography and book design, printing and binding, the rise and fall of publishing houses and periodicals, and the roles of authors and illustrators. It documents the ebb and flow of the book trade supplying a wide range of customers with products from almanacs to novels, bibles to erotica, and poetry to statistics.

Memoirs and Recollections of the Late Abraham Raimbach, Esq., Engraver

Born in London, Abraham Raimbach (1776–1843) was one of the most celebrated engravers of his time. Published in 1843, these memoirs recount his career and give expanded first-hand observations on contemporary artists and public figures. Included is an extensive account of his two months in Paris in 1802, including impressions of its people and food (on frog's legs: 'I did not much like the flavour'), together with details of the numerous works of art he viewed. He muses on the possible reasons for the higher social standing afforded to artists in France than in Britain, and seems concerned, as travellers are today, about how far his money will stretch whilst in France. Also included is a short biography of Raimbach's principal collaborator, the painter Sir David Wilkie, written by Raimbach's son. This memoir will be of interest to social and art historians of the early nineteenth century.

Cambridge University Press has long been a pioneer in the reissuing of out-of-print titles from its own backlist, producing digital reprints of books that are still sought after by scholars and students but could not be reprinted economically using traditional technology. The Cambridge Library Collection extends this activity to a wider range of books which are still of importance to researchers and professionals, either for the source material they contain, or as landmarks in the history of their academic discipline.

Drawing from the world-renowned collections in the Cambridge University Library, and guided by the advice of experts in each subject area, Cambridge University Press is using state-of-the-art scanning machines in its own Printing House to capture the content of each book selected for inclusion. The files are processed to give a consistently clear, crisp image, and the books finished to the high quality standard for which the Press is recognised around the world. The latest print-on-demand technology ensures that the books will remain available indefinitely, and that orders for single or multiple copies can quickly be supplied.

The Cambridge Library Collection will bring back to life books of enduring scholarly value (including out-of-copyright works originally issued by other publishers) across a wide range of disciplines in the humanities and social sciences and in science and technology.

Memoirs and Recollections of the Late Abraham Raimbach, Esq., Engraver

Including a Memoir of Sir David Wilkie

EDITED BY M. T. S. RAIMBACH

CAMBRIDGE
UNIVERSITY PRESS

CAMBRIDGE UNIVERSITY PRESS

Cambridge, New York, Melbourne, Madrid, Cape Town, Singapore,
São Paolo, Delhi, Dubai, Tokyo, Mexico City

Published in the United States of America by Cambridge University Press, New York

www.cambridge.org
Information on this title: www.cambridge.org/9781108027168

© in this compilation Cambridge University Press 2011

This edition first published 1843
This digitally printed version 2011

ISBN 978-1-108-02716-8 Paperback

MEMOIRS AND RECOLLECTIONS

OF THE LATE

ABRAHAM RAIMBACH, ESQ.

BATE'S PATENT ANAGLYPTOGRAPH.
ENGRAVED by FREEBAIRN.
J.E. CATTEAUX. from the Medallion by
CHEVALIER DE LA LEGION D'HONNEUR.

MEMOIRS AND RECOLLECTIONS

OF THE LATE

ABRAHAM RAIMBACH, ESQ.

ENGRAVER,

CORRESPONDING MEMBER OF THE INSTITUTE OF FRANCE,
AND HONORARY MEMBER OF THE ACADEMIES OF ARTS OF ST. PETERSBURGH,
GENEVA, AND AMSTERDAM.

INCLUDING A

MEMOIR OF SIR DAVID WILKIE, R.A.

EDITED BY

M. T. S. RAIMBACH, M.A.

"Nor does the chisel occupy alone
The power of Sculpture, but the style as much;
Each province of her art her equal care.
With nice incision of her guided steel,
She ploughs a brazen field, and clothes a soil
So sterile with what charms soe'er she will—
The richest scenery and the loveliest forms."

COWPER.

LONDON:

FREDERICK SHOBERL, JUNIOR,

Printer to His Royal Highness Prince Albert,

51, RUPERT STREET, HAYMARKET, 1843.

[Not Published.]

PREFATORY OBSERVATIONS.

Greenwich, 27th of March, 1836.

The following desultory notes, biographical and miscellaneous, have been put down at the earnest and repeated request of my eldest son. They can have little or no interest beyond the immediate family circle of the individual to whom they chiefly relate, and will probably be found scarcely worth the trouble of recording. I should merely wish to observe, in regard to the authenticity of the various circumstances detailed, that I have asserted nothing but what I knew of my own knowledge, or acquired from unquestionable authority ; and that I conscientiously believe that I have in no instance either exaggerated or " set down aught in malice," scrupulously adhering to the truth and nothing but the truth, as far as I knew it, in every case that came under my notice.

Whether the task prove irksome or agreeable in its execution, I shall at least have the pleasure of acceding to the wishes of one whose claims to my most affec- tionate regard I admit with proud satisfaction to be on every account entitled to the fullest acknowledg- ment.

ABRAHAM RAIMBACH.

The above prefatory notice sufficiently explains the immediate object with which these Memoirs were writ- ten. Believing that their interest would not be con- fined to the family alone, it was my intention at first to publish them in the usual manner. But not having succeeded in making any arrangement for that purpose, suitable either to my views or wishes, I adopted the more independent plan of printing a small edition at my own expense, for distribution amongst the friends of my late father, and such persons as a taste for art or the exercise of it as a profession may have rendered curious to know the toilsome path by which he arrived at eminence, and his opinions on subjects with which he was peculiarly conversant.

Nothing has been omitted that could be either interesting or instructive to the reader, nothing added but the few notes to which my initials are affixed, and a short Appendix containing three letters connected with the subject matter of the body of the work—one from Sir David Wilkie and two from Mr. Thomas Uwins.

My father has himself stated that he was never able to avail himself of any efficient assistance in the preparation or execution of the less important parts of his works, though often attempted in the earlier time of his career. I can add, of my own knowledge, that the series of engravings commonly known as the *Wilkie Prints* were entirely the work of his own hand, to which may perhaps in part be attributed their uniformity of excellence.

I am much indebted to my friend Mr. Bolton Corney for his kind assistance while the sheets were passing through the press, rendered doubly valuable by my necessary absence from London.

MICHAEL THOMSON SCOTT RAIMBACH.

H. M. S. Caledonia,
Devonport, 24 July, 1843.

MEMOIRS.

I was born in London, February 16th, 1776.[1] My father, a native of Switzerland,[2] came to England at the early age of twelve, and never afterwards quitted it. My mother was a Warwickshire woman, daughter of a farmer of the name of Butler, and descended by the female side, as was supposed, from the Burbages of Shakspere's time; one of whom, Will Burbage, according to the meagre traditions respecting our immortal bard, was his favourite player, friend, and companion. However this may have been, the virtues and qualities displayed by my mother in her humble station would have done honour to the highest pedigree. My father was of a quick and violent temper, which was invariably disarmed of all ill-effects by the just influence of my mother's gentleness, good sense, and discreet management. He was, however, a man of good and generous disposition, and of perfectly honest principles; while, combining with a certain originality of character, his occasional misapplication of words[3] in English, (to him a foreign

[1] In Cecil Court, St. Martin's Lane, Westminster.

[2] Of Crassier, between Geneva and Lausanne; in which latter places I have two or three cousins still living, (1836) whom I have seen in England at an early period of my life.

[3] The comic effect produced by this habit, aided as it was by the most earnest unconsciousness of manner, it is quite impossible to convey; but of the

B

language) though with no material defect of pronunciation,
rendered his familiar and judicious observations exceedingly
entertaining. He lived happily with my mother and was fond
of his children ; but, though I am bound equally to respect the
memory of both my parents, still that of my mother has always
commanded my more especial reverence. Her all-absorbing
affection for her offspring, her mildness of temper, the wisdom
of her precepts, and the force of her example, are, even to this
late time, constantly present to my recollection.

I am the eldest survivor of my family, two or three of the
children, my seniors, having died in early infancy, and myself
having narrowly escaped death by a fall from the nurse's arms
out of a second-floor window.[4] How numerous are the chances
against human life, from disease and accident, and what myriads
are prematurely swept away ! Looking at individual cases, it
would seem a matter of some difficulty to rear a human being
to maturity ; yet the most embarrassing problem of the day

nature of the *qui-pro-quo* the following may be taken as a sample :—
I had, when a boy, exceeded my usual allowance of pocket-money, in the
purchase of weekly periodicals, and had got into debt with my bookseller
to the amount of a few shillings, but which, small as it was, I saw no immediate prospect of liquidating, unless by the discontinuing of my *numbers*. This, of the two, being decidedly, in my opinion, the worst alter-
native, the other was adopted, of disclosing the circumstance, and making
an appeal to the bounty of my father. The appeal was admitted ; and I
was merely recommended not to run in debt, and never to *defray* any more
expenses than were necessary. Of course *incur* was the word meant.

[4] I was floated, in a manner, by my baby's long clothes, and my fall
broken by the leads of the first story. The servant girl rushed into the
room where my mother was sitting, exclaiming that she had killed the
child, quitted the house, and was never seen by her afterwards. I was not
materially hurt.

seems to be that of providing for the superabundance of the population.

The earliest impressions on the memory seem to be the most lasting. I distinctly remember the encampment of soldiery in St. James's Park, during the riots in 1780, and the panic-terror that prevailed in London, " frighted from its propriety." On one occasion, in particular, I recollect being awakened in the dead of night by a violent uproar, occasioned by the smashing of our windows and the yells of an infuriated mob rushing through the streets, calling upon the sleeping inhabitants to light up their rooms. The call was obeyed by my father as promptly as was possible, though with considerable danger to himself, from the stones that were thrown.

A somewhat precocious fondness for reading, and the desire of my parents to give their children an education which might qualify them for a step in advance of their own humble station, led to my being kept constantly at school, notwithstanding their poverty, till I was thirteen years old. With the exception of about a twelvemonth passed at Highgate, my book-learning, such as it is, was obtained at the Library School of St. Martin's, under the mastership of Mr. Pownall. Among my schoolfellows, of names since known to the public, the following may be enumerated : Henry Winchester, (afterwards lord mayor of London) Charles Mathews, William Lovegrove, (actors) John Richter, (tried for high treason, with Hardy and H. Tooke, 1794) Henry Richter, (artist) William Woodburne, (now a picture-dealer) Alexander Copland, government contractor for buildings. Liston, the comedian, was for a time connected with the establishment, either as master or assistant. This happened long after I had left, and, of course, before he became celebrated as a player, though not before he had commenced the thorny and up-hill path of that difficult and uncertain profession. The qualities that indicate the future actor are not, perhaps, developed so early as may be sometimes witnessed in other pursuits connected with the imitative arts. Certain it is that neither Mathews nor Lovegrove, in their schoolboy days, showed any of that *vis comica* which in after-years used to set the house in a roar.

Men are apt to look back on their school-days as a period of unmingled enjoyment, or at least of great comparative happiness. Is there not some self-delusion in this? Are not a schoolboy's troubles in due proportion to his power of bearing them? Undoubtedly, if we could re-live that portion of our existence, with the after-acquired experience of the miseries of human life, there might be some grounds for the notion; but, as it is, it seems to me an opinion founded in error.

A fondness for pictures and prints, together with a certain degree of readiness and a good deal of perseverance in the practice of drawing, pointed out very early to my friends some branch of the fine arts as a congenial and suitable profession for me, and thereby preferring it to the study of the law, as it is called, in an attorney's office, which had been first thought of. I do not know how it happened that engraving was chosen as the most fitting department of art for me to pursue, unless it was suggested by the cleverness with which I used to dig, with a cobbler's awl, upon a marble, ground flat upon the pavement, the initial letters of my schoolfellows' names. I rather wonder that this did not lead to my being made a seal-cutter, or carver of stone. Engraving was, however, determined on; and, in the beginning of the year 1789, application was personally made by my father to the two most eminent men in the art, Mr. Sharp and Mr. Heath; the former of whom professed himself to be unwilling to take a pupil, as he had it in contemplation to go abroad (which, by the by, he never did) ; and the latter stated (what I believe was true enough) that he was already over-stocked with pupils.[5] An engagement was ultimately entered into with Mr. Hall ; and, after a short interval of probation, articles for seven years were finally agreed on and signed by the respective parties, and witnessed by Mr. Hall's son-in-law, Stephen Storace, the musical composer. The conditions of the engagement were, that I was to breakfast and dine at Mr. Hall's, and sleep at home ; my friends to pay a premium of fifty pounds. This sum was only half the usual fee ; but my father pleaded poverty in his so peculiarly odd manner, that it could not be easily resisted.[6]

I have never considered it a matter to be regretted that the application to Sharp and Heath did not succeed, though their professional talents were doubtless greatly superior to those of Hall. So little is to be derived, in the acquirement of an art, from the skill and ability of a master, however distinguished he may be, that the degree of his eminence I take to be of very small importance to the pupil. In my own case, I am disposed

---

[5] A day or two afterwards, my father, in the simplicity of his heart, sent me to Mr. Heath, saying that he might perhaps take a fancy to me when he saw me. I did not at all relish this commission, which was to see Mr. Heath, and inquire whether he wanted a pupil. I was received with civility, or rather with kindness ; though he appeared evidently surprised at the singularity of the message, which I delivered to him personally, in the passage of his house, No. 42, Newman Street.

[6] After settling the terms, Mr. Hall offered to make the time of payment convenient to circumstances, suggesting a bill at a distant date. It was quite characteristic in my father's instantly giving a cheque on Drummond's for the amount, to the great and not disagreeable surprise of the other party.

mainly to limit the benefits of pupilage to the constant and
regular habits of assiduous attention, induced by example and
enforced by authority. Almost all beyond the mere routine
the student must seek out for himself. The very best of teaching can do little more than indicate the means of success—the
path which leads to distinction : it cannot convey originality,
or the power of forming original or new combinations ; and
without these, or some such faculties, nothing beyond mediocrity can result. All true excellence in art is, in my humble
opinion, to be chiefly attributed to an early conviction of the
inadequacy of all means of improvement, in comparison with
that of self-acquired knowledge.

Hall, though not of first-rate powers, was an artist of very
respectable abilities. He was born at Wivenhoe, in Essex,
anno 1739, and became a pupil of Simon Francis Ravenet,[7] an
ingenious Frenchman, who had settled in London. The unfortunate William Wynne Ryland,[8] afterwards executed at Tyburn

[7] Ravenet produced nothing very remarkable, unless his pupil Ryland may
be so considered. I recollect, however, a small portrait that he engraved
of himself that had great cleverness, and was replete with true French
character. It was inscribed, " S. F. Ravenet, gravé par lui-même, d'après
un tableau peint par son ami Zoffany." The picture was no doubt exquisite.

[8] William Wynne Ryland, born 1732, was the son of a printer in the Old
Bailey, and, after the expiration of his term with Ravenet, went to Paris,
and studied under Boucher, the painter, and Lebas, the engraver. On his
return to England, he engraved the portrait of Lord Bute, from a picture
by Allan Ramsay, (son of the poet of *The Gentle Shepherd*) was patronized by his lordship, afterwards engraved the whole length of Queen Charlotte and her infant, (George, Prince of Wales, afterwards George the
Fourth) and received a pension of £200 a year. Ramsay, the painter, is
supposed to be characterized by Smollett, in the tenth chapter of the second

for forgery of an India bond, was his fellow-student in the same school of engraving. Hall had previously worked at Sir Stephen Jansen's (I believe) manufactory of painted porcelain at Chelsea. He studied under Ravenet only for a short term, and at the end of that engagement was certainly but very inadequately qualified to get his living by the art, judging from his early productions ; the more especially as he was gentlemanly in his habits and connexions, and somewhat disposed to extravagance in dress, for which, as he told me, he was exposed to the censure of his companion, Ryland, who was of quakerish simplicity in his personal appearance.

Hall, however, by dint of perseverance and good conduct, and notwithstanding his marriage at the age of twenty-two, lived in great respectability, obtained a fair reputation as an artist, and brought up a numerous family in credit and in comfort. His eldest son George, educated at St. Paul's School, is now master of Pembroke College, Oxford. His youngest son was brought up as an attorney, and was not prosperous. His four daughters married respectively Mr. Aspinall, a Birmingham manufacturer, Mr. Joseph Burchell, the deputy sheriff of London, Stephen Storace, the celebrated musical composer, and the Rev. Rann Kennedy, master of the free-school at Birming-

volume of Roderick Random, under the name of Slyboot. The Rylands were singularly unfortunate. One of the family, Joseph, brother of William, had very narrowly escaped the fate which afterwards befel his brother, as I was informed by Mr. Hall, though I did not learn the particulars. He (Joe Ryland) was remarkably handsome in person in early life ; and indeed when I saw him, then an elderly man, there were evident remains of that symmetry of form and those "hyacinthine locks" which led painters to choose him as a model for angels. The widow and daughter of W. W. Ryland kept a print-shop in Bond Street, in my remembrance.

ham.   Of Storace[9] I had opportunities of seeing a good deal
at Hall's table, as I had also of Aspinall and Burchell : Kennedy was after my time, and of course I know nothing of him
personally, but his reputation is that of a man of literature and
taste.   His sons have " earned golden opinions " at Cambridge

[9] Stephen Storace was the son of an Italian, born in London, and brother
to the eminent singer of the Opera House and Drury-lane Theatre, Signora
Storace.   A current joke of the time insisted upon the omission of the letter *t* as the true reading of the name, which had been altered in deference
to British ears.   Stephen Storace was unquestionably a man of genius.
His musical education had been completed in a conservatorio at Naples,
and, had life been spared to him, he would doubtless have taken a very high
place indeed in the list of English composers.   He died at the age of thirty-
three, with a reputation already well established.   The music of Mahmoud
and of the Iron Chest (the rehearsal of which latter he attended during his
last illness, wrapped up in flannel, and carried on to the stage in a sedan,)
were afterwards published by subscription.   I lent and *lost* my copy, presented to me by the widow.   Storace in person was of a tall and handsome
figure, but his face had suffered considerably from smallpox.   His intellectual qualities were by no means confined to his knowledge of music.
He was distinguished for acuteness of observation and soundness of judgment.   His wit, keenness of perception, and ready fluency of remark, rendered him admirable in familiar conversation.   His manners, though perfectly gentlemanly, were somewhat haughty, reserved, and unconciliatory
with strangers.   I engraved his portrait for the title-page of the publication
mentioned above from a miniature by Arland (a Swiss) painted after his
death, and but very little resembling the man himself.   Storace, after
having overcome the great difficulties that almost every professional man
has to encounter before he can emerge from poverty and obscurity, was
on the high road to fortune when so prematurely cut off.   But at that time,
musical composition was much better remunerated than it appears to be at
present.   For the music of *The Haunted Tower*, his first work of importance, he received, I believe, £300 of Longman and Broderip, and for
that of the *Siege of Belgrade*, £500, from Dale, a music-seller in Oxford
Street, whose daughter was married to Steibelt.

by their talents. Burchell was succeeded in his office of deputy
sheriff by one of his sons, who had previously married his cousin, Mary Aspinall. The Aspinalls had been unfortunate, but of
their ultimate destiny I am ignorant. Few men of Hall's station and profession have done so well with their children. He
forms indeed, in this respect, a strong contrast with his illustrious contemporary and friend, Woollet, whose widow and
daughters were in a great degree dependent upon public bene-
volence for support, and whose only son threw away all his
advantages and neglected the fairest opportunities, to become
an outcast and a vagabond. I regret never having seen Woollet,
but he died a few years before I went to engraving, from the
effect of an accident, unskilfully treated by an ignorant pretender.
John Hunter was called in, but too late.

I have always been disposed to reckon among the chief advantages I derived from being placed with Mr. Hall the opportunity it afforded me of getting occasionally a glimpse of men
distinguished in some way or other by talent or notoriety.
Sheridan came twice or thrice, once with Joseph Richardson,
author of *The Fugitive*, during the engraving of his portrait ;
and my memory dwells with pleasure to this hour on the recollection of his having said a few kindly and encouraging words
to me, a boy, drawing at the time in the study. I was, however, most struck with what seemed in such a man an undue
and unbecoming anxiety about his good looks in the portrait
to be executed. The efflorescence in his face had been indicated
by Sir Joshua in his picture, not, it may be presumed, *à bon gré*,
on the part of Sheridan, and it was strongly evident that he
deprecated its transfer to the print. I need scarcely observe
that Hall set his mind at ease on this point ; but I could not
but wonder that a matter that might be excused in the other

sex should have had power to ruffle the thoughts of the great
wit, poet, and orator, of the age. Kemble,[10] from his friendship
and intimacy with Storace, was also an occasional visiter, and
of course formed an object of great interest with me. Hall had
had in his time the advantage of a personal introduction to
Garrick ; and this circumstance, with his fondness to the last of
theatrical entertainments, afforded me, through conversation
with him, a tolerable insight into the state of dramatic performances immediately preceding my own time, as well as some

[10] Kemble, who, from the grandeur of his figure, the expression of his face,
and the grace of his action, was distinguishable by the commonest observer
from the multitude, could not fail, combined as they were with the *prestige* as
the representative of heroes, kings, and cardinals, to impress strongly my
young, unsophisticated mind with respect and admiration. He seemed, to
my boyish judgment, a man unlike any other of the species. The measured
solemnity of his ordinary enunciation, coupled with the naturally hollow
tones of his voice, and the highly artificial habitual manner of his general
demeanour, does now, after years of after-experience and reflection, fully justify my early opinion. He was, as I believe almost all of his profession are,
the *actor off* the stage as well as *on*. Of his conversation I remember but
little, though I will not say that it was not worth remembering. Indeed, in
the common and trivial intercourse of ordinary society, it is no imputation on
any man, whatever may be his qualities and station, if he do not reach the
standard which our imagination may have formed of him. He never, either
on or off the stage, appeared to forget for a moment that he was acting a part,
or to lose sight of the part he was acting. He had never seen Garrick ;
and his style of art was probably as diametrically opposed as it is possible
to conceive to the natural, unexaggerated, and captivating manner, as I
have heard it described, of his unequalled predecessor. It is, however, but
justice to declare, for my own part, that I have never seen, nor can I imagine,
any thing in acting more highly studied and finished in execution than
Kemble's performances of Cato, Coriolanus, the Duke, (Measure for Measure) Jacques, Leon, (Rule a Wife and have a Wife) the Stranger, Pen-
ruddock, Octavian, Rolla, &c.

slight means of comparison with its then existing condition ; and I should not hesitate to declare that the mode of art introduced by Kemble was utterly inefficient to sustain the shock of a return to the principles of truth, nature, and feeling. I have lived, indeed, to witness the eclipse, if not the total extinction of the Kemble school, (as followed out by Young, Charles Kemble, and others) by the genius, taste, and energy of Kean.

Among the persons I had opportunities of seeing frequently at Mr. Hall's was his god-daughter, Anna Selina Fischer, better known by her family name of Signora Storace.[11] She had married, when very young, a famous German fiddler, Dr. Fischer, from whom she soon separated, as was said, of course, by her family and friends, in consequence of his ill-usage. In revenge, or, to speak more charitably, to indemnify herself perhaps, she attached herself, first to Mr. Attwood, the present composer and organist ; then to Mr. Brian Barret, the wax-

[11] Signora Storace, which name she retained, notwithstanding her marriage, was highly popular, and was doubtless a very finished singer and accomplished musician. She had also many admirers of her powers as a comic actress : it might be from deficiency of taste in me, but I confess that I was not of the number. There was in her acting, according to my notions, a coarseness and vulgarity of manner, which, without being natural, was, in my mind, repugnant to all ideas of grace, delicacy, or refinement. Whether or not she had imbibed her style in the Italian buffo school I cannot pretend to determine ; but it was certainly very different from any thing I had ever witnessed on the English stage, or, indeed, on any other. It had perhaps the merit of being original and unimitated, if not, as was said by her admirers, inimitable. In person she was rather below the middle stature, and somewhat inclined to *embonpoint*. Her voice was very deep, powerful, and of great compass, perfectly under her command, never out of tune, and remarkably articulate, both in singing and speaking.

chandler, who afterwards committed suicide ; and, finally, not to
name some casual and incidental *passages of love*, to Braham, by
whom she had a son, now a prebendary of Canterbury, who in his
turn quitted her : a mortification so severe as to have, as it has
been stated, ultimately broken her heart. However that may
have been, certain it is that she died soon after Braham's marriage with his present wife.

When first placed with Mr. Hall, I could draw, perhaps,
better than the generality of boys, and was soon put forward to
that which was serviceable to my master. One of the first
occasions that occurred of my rendering valuable assistance
was when I had been about a twelvemonth at engraving. On
the publication of the large plate by Bartolozzi of the Death
of the Earl of Chatham, it was unaccompanied by the outline
of the heads usually issued in such cases as a key or explanation to the portraits. This, by the way, was supposed to
have arisen from the characteristic Yankee astuteness of Copley,[12] who could not in decency have charged his numerous
subscribers to the print, (a high-priced one at the time) *on its
delivery*, an additional three shillings and sixpence (which he
did afterwards) for the explanatory etching. However, he

---

[12] John Singleton Copley, father of the present Lord Lyndhurst, was,
like West, a native of America. He was born, I believe, in Boston, where
also was born, if I am not mistaken, his truly illustrious son, the present
Lord Lyndhurst. He had several daughters, but I never heard that he
had any other son. He resided in George Street, Hanover Square, in the
house afterwards long occupied by Lord Lyndhurst. About the year 1791,
I was sent there several times on business, and saw the ladies of the family
occasionally, but the son was probably away for his education. The plate
of the Death of Lord Chatham was printed by Madame Hocquet, a Frenchwoman, on Copley's premises, in George Street, the coach-house and
stabling being made available for the purpose.

applied to Mr. Hall, and finally the execution of it fell to my lot. I naturally felt diffident in undertaking a task that seemed beyond my powers, but was encouraged to make the attempt, and succeeded tolerably well, as may be seen at the present time in the National Gallery, where an impression hangs suspended under the original picture. This, my first money-getting service, produced Hall fifteen guineas.

The Death of Lord Chatham by Bartolozzi is too well known to need description. Although a work of great ability and immense labour, it has never become a standard, or at all a popular print. It was many years in hand, and the price agreed upon with Copley (2000 guineas, as I understood) was nearly expended by Bartolozzi on assistance, which proved, for the most part, according to his account, worse than none. Testolini,[13] a fellow-countryman, was employed on it for three or four years, and, as I heard him state, to the entire satisfaction, as expressed by his principal, during its progress; but their engagement terminated in a quarrel, and Bartolozzi erased much of what Testolini had done. Delattre,[14] the ordinary and regular assistant of Bartolozzi, also contributed his aid, and was afterwards commissioned by Copley to make a smaller engraving, a copy of the larger, for which he engaged to pay him five or six hundred guineas, but afterwards refused to receive the plate,

[13] Testolini afterwards kept a print-shop in Cornhill. He came to England at the same time, I believe, with his more celebrated friend and fellow-countryman, Schiavonetti.

[14] Jean Marie Delattre, a Frenchman, born at Abbeville, was brought to England by William Wynne Ryland, and, after his death, was chiefly employed by Bartolozzi. He was much respected as an individual, and is still living, (1836) at a very advanced age, a pensioner on the late Peter Herve's excellent society for the relief of the middle classes.

on the plea of gross imperfection in its execution. This led ultimately (1801) to a lawsuit,[15] which excited great interest in the little world of art, and ended in favour of Delattre, to whom the jury gave a verdict for the whole amount of his claim. The plate, however, though paid for, was never published. The motive which influenced Copley in having a smaller engraving made was with the view of preventing surreptitious copies being circulated, to the detriment of the larger one, from the successful sale of which he expected extraordinary results ; in which, I think, he must have been greatly disappointed. The last time I saw Copley was in 1812, at Wilkie's exhibition in Pall Mall. The family was latterly supported chiefly by the son.

[15] The trial took place in the Court of King's Bench, Westminster, in 1801, before Lord Kenyon, Chief Justice. The counsel for Copley were Messrs. Erskine and Garrow, &c.; for Delattre, Mr. Law, Attorney-General, (afterwards Lord Ellenborough) who made decidedly the best speech of the day. The evidence, as was remarked by Lord Kenyon in summing up, was of an equal number, thirteen on each side, and consisted of painters, engravers, and publishers: the painters ranging generally on the side of Copley, and the engravers on that of Delattre. Of the painters were West, Opie, Hoppner, Beechey, and Bourgeois; of the engravers were Bartolozzi, Bromley, Landseer, Neagle, &c. Copley's son appeared in the witness-box, for the purpose of proving some fact, making the chain of evidence complete. The future Lord Lyndhurst was then a smart-looking young man, about twenty-eight or twenty-nine, with powdered hair, buckskin breeches, and top-boots ; and, I dare say, little thought at the time of what Fortune had in store for him. I was a mere looker-on, and, after the trial, dined with the winning party at the Spring Garden coffee-house. An attempt was made to record the event, by the publication of the trial; but, no previous arrangement having been made, and the desultory notes of the reporters present not being found sufficient, the scheme fell to the ground. A " Society of Engravers," however, grew out of these circumstances, which had a languishing existence for a few years, and then silently gave up the ghost.

To return to my pupilage. When I was articled with Mr. Hall, he had just completed the engraving of Cromwell dissolving the Long Parliament, from the picture by West, painted for Lord Grosvenor. This was the third and last plate of that size that Hall executed. Its companion, Charles the Second landing at Dover on his Restoration, begun by Woollet, was finished by Sharp.[16] The moderate degree of success which

---

[16] Woollet and Sharp; two of the greatest names that adorn the history of the art. It would be presumption in me to attempt to characterize the surpassing excellence of these admirable artists. The versatility, truth, force, and harmony, displayed in the works of Woollet leave him without a rival; while Sharp, by taste, feeling, vigour, and freedom of execution, is justly entitled to take one of the foremost places in the very first rank of eminence. Woollet died before my time; but with Sharp I was not unacquainted. Of Woollet, therefore, I can only repeat what I heard from his friend and associate, Hall, who was united with him and West in the publication of the plates of La Hogue and Battle of the Boyne, &c. In person Woollet was rather below the middle stature, and extremely simple and unpretending in manner and demeanour. He had been apprenticed to a general engraver in Cheapside. His great works were executed at his house, the corner of Charlotte and North Streets. The house has undergone much alteration of late years; but, till a comparatively recent period, the window of his workroom, which he had adapted to his purpose, and had a northern aspect, remained unaltered. He was accustomed, on the completion of a plate, to assemble his family on the landing-place of his study, (the first-floor) and all give three cheers. He was intimate with Parsons, the celebrated comedian, who had a taste for the arts, and they occasionally smoked their pipes together. Woollet was a man of integrity, candour, and liberality, worthy of his elevated station as an artist. I have seen a letter of his, in which he bore the highest testimony of his admiration and respect for the talents of his then considered rival, Bartolozzi. He died about the age of fifty, leaving a widow, a son, and two daughters. He had realized but a small property. Sharp I knew personally. He was as notorious for singularity of character as he was celebrated for talent in his

16   MEMOIRS.

attended the publication of this pair of prints did not encourage
Hall to undertake any other of similar dimensions. During
the time that I was with him, he was chiefly occupied on plates
for Macklin's Bible, Bowyer's edition of Hume's *History of
England*, Woodmason's *Shakspere*, with some small book-
plates occasionally for Bell's *British Theatre*. My business was
to advance as far as I could with these; but I was very soon
impressed with the conviction of the importance of drawing as
a necessary means for any chance of distinction, and therefore
all my available time was devoted to its study and practice.
This consisted chiefly of the hours before eight o'clock in the
morning and after six o'clock in the evening, at my father's re-

profession. After his apprenticeship, with a man of the name of Longmate,
he began as a writing and heraldry engraver in Doctors' Commons, where
he kept a small shop, of which there is a card extant of his own execution.
He afterwards engraved a good many book-plates for the *Novelist's Magazine, English Theatre*, &c. His first great work (perhaps the greatest)
was The Doctors of the Church, &c., which was followed by the splendid
portrait of John Hunter, The sortie of Gibraltar, King Lear, and a great
number of other fine works. He was engaged by Copley to engrave his
picture of the Destruction of the Floating Batteries, (exhibited in a large
tent in the Green Park, by express permission of George III.) which, after
the lapse of twenty years, was published, but with little success. Sharp
was said to have dissipated a decent patrimonial fortune in the indulgence
and pursuit of his wild vagaries. He was a proselyte of the insane prophet,
Richard Brothers, and of Johanna Southcote, to the very last, engraving
their portraits in testimony of his faith in their prophecies. He was impli-
cated slightly in the affair of Hardy and Horne Tooke, who were tried
for high treason in 1794. In his ordinary conversation he was shrewd and
intelligent, but with a general tinge of eccentricity. He died at Chiswick,
about the age of seventy, and left little or no property. He was about the
middle stature, corpulent, and with a head worthy the sculptor's art, as is
proved by Chantrey's fine bust of him.

sidence, and was usually occupied in drawing from small copies of the antique figures, in plaster of Paris. I was desirous, during my pupilage, of drawing at the Royal Academy ; but, as there appeared to be an unwillingness on the part of Mr. Hall to consent, it was not urged. I do not know that there was any other reason for the objection, on his part, but the apprehension of its interfering, however little it might be, with the due prosecution of my labours for him. Be that as it may, I was obliged to forego my inclination till the expiration of my articles, in 1796, when I immediately entered as a probationer, by the introduction of Mr. Edward Edwards, associate and teacher of perspective in the Royal Academy. He was an old friend and constant visiter at Mr. Hall's, and had repeatedly recommended the measure to my adoption. I was, however, better qualified to profit by the advantages of study at the Royal Academy from the delay that occurred and the use I had made of the interval. The Mr. Edwards here mentioned, and Ozias Humphrey, the miniature and crayon painter, were personal friends of Mr. Hall, both of whom I had many opportunities of seeing at the house. Edwards was small and deformed in figure, with strong marked features and bushy eyebrows, of which latter he seemed to be rather proud. He was a man of considerable acquirements, much diversity of knowledge, and a very respectable degree of literary talent ; but he had not attained excellence in any of the various branches of art he had pursued. He had had the advantage, if it be one, of a wealthy patron in Ralph Udney, Esquire, who sent him to Italy, and liberally enabled him to pass some years at Rome. The lessons he gave on perspective in the Academy were probably more practically useful to the young men than were the professor's (Turner) lectures at an after-time. He thought himself ill-used, of course, at not

C

being elected a Royal Academician.   Ozias Humphrey was by
profession a miniature-painter, one of the very best of his time,
dividing with Cosway the patronage of the beauty, rank, and
fashion of the day.   His sight became weak, and he discontinued miniature-portraits, but turned his attention to crayon-
painting, and completely eclipsed his only competitor, Russel.
Humphrey was a highly-accomplished artist, and in his manners quite a gentleman of the old school.   Upcott, the secretary of the London Institution, Finsbury, is in possession of
many of his drawings.

Mr. Heath,[17] without being intimate, was on friendly terms

---

[17] James Heath was born in London, about the year 1758, and died
1834. He was a pupil of Joseph Collyer, a respectable engraver, whose
principal work was a large plate of the Assemblage of the Irish Volun-
teers in Dublin, and who afterwards chiefly employed himself in small portraits in the chalk manner. Heath complained, I believe, of the severity
of Collyer's treatment of him, and his rigid enforcement of close application. Without entering upon Collyer's motives, there can be little doubt
but that Heath derived the greatest advantage from this circumstance,
inasmuch as that high degree of mechanical execution, which constitutes
one of the fascinating qualities of Heath's engraving, may fairly be deduced
from it. His numerous early book-plates for *Bell's Poets, The Novelist's
Magazine*, &c., exhibit a display of tasteful ingenuity till then unknown in
this department of art. Its popularity afforded Heath an opportunity of
turning his talent to account, of which he did not fail to profit. He constantly employed a considerable number of assistants, from whose labours
he derived great pecuniary advantages, and willingly sacrificed a portion
of his reputation as an artist to his desire of becoming a rich man. Hence
many of the works bearing his name contain but little of his labour, and
are far below that standard of tasteful and elegant execution in which his
excellence was acknowledged. His larger productions, the Riot in Broad
Street, Death of Major Pierson, and Death of Nelson, do not maintain a
very high character, though it must, I think, be admitted that the small

with Hall, and presented him with a proof, on India paper, of the Riot in Broad Street. He occasionally called, and was admitted to the study, much to my gratification ; as, from my unbounded admiration of his talent, I felt of course interest as well as curiosity in observing his personal appearance, and listening to his conversation with Mr. Hall.

The portrait of Sheridan, from Sir Joshua Reynolds, was Hall's first work, after I had been fixed with him. He published it himself, but it had but little success. On its termination, Macklin, in my hearing, offered 450 guineas for the plate, but Hall stood out for 500, (observing that Macklin had given the larger sum for the portrait of Lord Mansfield, in the chalk manner, by Bartolozzi) and the negotiation went off, very unfortunately for Hall, as I do not believe it ever produced him half the money. Mr. Hall undertook no other large plates ; though another subject from West was talked of from time to time. Before the termination of my pupilage, his health began to decline, and he died not many months after I left him, 1796, aged about fifty-seven. I should mention that, in 1793, he engraved a portrait of the admiral Lord Hawke, from a picture by Cotes ;[18] but, warned by the ill success of his print of Sheridan, he was only induced to undertake it by a considerable subscription previously in hand ; for which he was indebted to the

figures in the first named are of exquisite beauty. Heath accepted the diploma of Associate Engraver in the Royal Academy, to the great vexation and surprise of Sharp and Hall, who had invariably spurned it, considering, as did Woollet and Strange, that it was injurious to the profession, and degrading to the individual.

[18] This picture is now in the Hall of Greenwich Hospital. Cotes was professionally a crayon-painter, but occasionally produced pictures in oil. Crayon-painting seems now to be nearly a lost art.

zealous exertions of his constant friend, Commodore Locker,[19]
late lieutenant-governor of Greenwich Hospital. The plate,
however, was never published, having been purchased by Lord
Hawke, son of the admiral, for distribution among his private
friends. The numerous subscribers, chiefly naval officers, were
of course supplied with their prints, having previously paid for
them. Sir John Jervis, (Earl St. Vincent) Admiral Edwards,
(Toby Edwards,[20] as he was called by his naval friends) and
other eminent sea-officers, who also interested themselves in this
portrait, I remember to have seen together during its progress.
The study was on the upper story of the house ; and, though
up three pair of stairs, it was, I believe, considered, and was
certainly intended by Mr. Hall, as rather a favour to be admitted. Among others, I may name having seen John Ireland,[21] Hogarth's annotator; George Steevens,[22] the com-

19 Commodore Locker, Lieutenant-Governor of Greenwich Hospital, had
been one of Hawke's lieutenants. Commodore Locker was, as many naval
officers are, an amateur of the arts, and rather a frequent visiter to Mr.
Hall's study. He was a good specimen of the old English sea-officer —
kind-hearted, dignified, and free from all affectation. I have always borne
his memory in respect. His youngest son, Edward, is now (1836) one of
the Commissioners of Greenwich Hospital.

20 Sir J. Jervis, to my juvenile observation, contrasted strongly with
his accompanying friend, Admiral Edwards. The former was refined
and polished in manner, while Edwards seemed to me the *beau-ideal* of a
thorough-bred and born seaman, large in person, blunt in his address,
and loud, hoarse, and decided in speech.

21 John Ireland had been a watch-maker. He was a thin, consumptive-
looking man, with a soft, drawling manner of speaking, that savoured
strongly of affectation.

22 George Steevens was said to be a personally vain man, habitually
contemplating with great complacency the reflection of his features in any
looking-glass that was within his view.

mentator on Shakespeare; Hoole,[23] the translator of Ariosto;
Barrow,[24] now Sir John Barrow; the two Hickeys, the one a
portrait-painter, the other a sculptor; Alexander, the draughtsman; Sir Richard Worsley; Woodmason; West;[25] Opie;
Northcote; Flaxman; Westall; Tomkins,[26] the writing-
master; Baker, the laceman of St. Paul's Churchyard, famous
in his day as a print-collector; Kelly, the singer;[27] and
Slingsby, the dancer.[28]

In August, 1796, my engagement with Mr. Hall terminated,
and, as the period drew near, I felt greatly and, I may say, not
unbecomingly anxious as to my future prospects. The war of

[23] Hoole was a clerk in the India House. He was uncle to Anker Smith,
the engraver.

[24] Barrow, Hickey the painter, and Alexander, went with Lord Macart-
ney's embassy to China. Barrow was of gentlemanly address and handsome person, Hickey an indifferent portrait-painter, and his brother a
rather clever sculptor. They were both men of education and polished
manners. Alexander was an expert draughtsman; good-tempered, intelligent, and unpresuming. He afterwards had the office of Keeper of the
Prints in the British Museum.

[25] West, Opie, Northcote, Flaxman, Westall, are names too well known
to need any remark.

[26] Tomkins was a favourable specimen of the old school in his appearance. He preserved till the last the costume of the early part of George
the Third's reign. Both he and Baker had been intimate with Woollet,
and possessed most of his finest works.

[27] Kelly was an accomplished musician. As a singer he had to struggle
against the insurmountable objection of a harsh, unpleasing voice.

[28] Slingsby had at this time quitted the stage, and taught dancing, in
which occupation he was much encouraged. He was a small, compact,
well-made, active Irishman, retaining a good deal of his original brogue, a
great flow of spirits, and much humour. His success in the comic parts was so
great as to cause, it was said, considerable jealousy on the part of Vestris,
" le *Diou* de la Danse," as he, in his Gascon accent, pronounced himself.

the French revolution was raging in all its fury ; and the nature of the contest, absorbing all men's thoughts and calling on all men's exertions, left but little opportunity for the cultivation of the peaceful arts. Every thing connected with them was, of course, at the lowest ebb—so low, indeed, that I remember, during Mr. Pitt's administration, the members and associates of the Royal Academy were expressly exempted from the operation of some war-tax, then levied, in consideration of the abject and almost expiring state to which the fine arts had been reduced. I forget the name of the tax in question, but have a distinct recollection of the fact stated, and, moreover, that it excited no feelings of dissatisfaction whatever in the community at large, so universally known was the destitute condition of the artists in general. I well knew that I had the kindest of parents,[29] who never were and never would be backward in affording me every assistance in their power ; but I equally felt it my duty to be a burthen to them no longer, more especially after what, with but slender means, they had already done for me, and had still to do for their younger children. Indeed, I must in justice say, at the risk of being set down as one of the *laudatores temporis acti*, that, in my early time, the young men were generally influenced by that just pride of independence which leads to a reliance solely upon self-exertion. With these sentiments, it will be readily believed that I spared no pains in seeking for

[29] I had taken a handsome first-floor in the house of Mr. Edwards, a surveyor, No. 13, Upper Titchfield Street, (now Cirencester Place) which my father had liberally furnished for me, supplying me at the same time with an excellent mahogany working-table, which has been my constant companion for forty years (I am now writing on it—1836). Edwards married, in 1801, a sister of Mazzinghi, the musical-composer, when I removed to Charles Street, Middlesex Hospital.

employment ; and, as the booksellers were at this time the only patrons (such as they were) of engraving, by the decoration, with little vignettes, of small volumes of poetry, plays, &c., I made assiduous application in every quarter where I thought there was the slightest probability of a successful result. I need scarcely add that I met with many mortifying refusals ; but, at length, after some week or ten days' painful suspense, I received a note from a bookseller to whom I had applied, desiring me to call on him in Piccadilly, with a view to a commission he had for me. I obtained the commission, though nothing was arranged or even hinted at respecting terms. The bookseller was Stockdale,[30] (father of the Stockdale of Harriette Wilson notoriety) and the engraving a figure from a drawing by Metz, of a Maroon chief, Leonard Parkinson, for Bryan Edwards's *History of the Maroon War*. This, my first start, was rather an inauspicious one, inasmuch as Stockdale refused to pay the sum I demanded, (six guineas) offering me two guineas, which I, in my turn, somewhat indignantly refused in a letter which appeared to nettle the old man extremely, as coming from a youth to whom he had shewn himself favourably disposed. The matter was, however, settled, I cannot say amicably, but without litigation, by means of a friend of both parties. He decided very judiciously I am *now* inclined to think, though, at the time, neither of the disputants was quite satisfied by his award. I

---

[30] John Stockdale, a respectable bookseller, was a Yorkshireman, and had been, I believe, a furrier. He was, *mutatis mutandis*, what Murray of Albemarle Street is at present, the publisher for the government party. I remember an admirable caricature of him by Gillray, in which he is represented at the bar of Bow Street for an assault, or some slight matter. The caricature was once in my possession, but has, with many other things more regretted, disappeared, I don't know how.

received four guineas for the plate, retaining, as of right, my indignant feelings towards my adversary, as a kind of set-off against the mortification of the diminished price.[31] The mediator

---

[31] The following letter of Mr. Stockdale's, relative to the transaction mentioned in the text, and the rough draught of the note from my father, I found among his papers.—M. T. S. R.

(No. 1.)

" Mr. Stockdale's compliments to Mr. Raimbach, assures him that he never was more surprised than by his note of this day, as he did not expect that he would have asked more than two guineas.

" Mr. S. has reason to be very glad that he has not proceeded with the view, as he fixed no price, under the idea that he would be reasonable in his charge. That not being the case, he begs to have the plate and drawing returned by the bearer.

" Mr. S. has hitherto had a very good opinion of Mr. Raimbach, but, from his note, strongly suspects he must have consulted some very unconscionable engraver. If the figure done were to be six guineas, it is not improbable that he would charge for the view six and twenty on the same principle. A few impressions shall of course be at Mr. R.'s service.

" Piccadilly, Nov. 30, 1796."

(No. 2.)
" Sir,
" I am very sorry that the note I sent to you yesterday should have occasioned any surprise, and I can assure you that I was myself much astonished when I understood that you expected to be asked no more than two guineas for the produce of three weeks' labour. With respect to the suspicion you entertain of my having consulted some very unconscionable engraver, I beg leave to inform you that I was regulated in my charge by one in whose favour I have heard you express yourself in strong terms of approbation. I should be sorry to forfeit the good opinion of any one, more especially of a gentleman who has hitherto behaved with more than common civility; but I must be allowed to say, that I would decline any man's favour who would wish to reduce the value of my labour to the level of blacking shoes, or sweeping the streets. If there should still exist a difference of opinion

was Mr. Philip Audinet,[32] my predecessor in Mr. Hall's study, a respectable and well-meaning man, of moderate pretensions as an artist.

Soon after, by dint of repeatedly applying, I obtained a small commission from Cooke of Paternoster Row, a publisher of miniature editions of the works of the poets and novelists. A little picture of Kirk, from the *Tales of the Genii*, formed my *coup-d'essai*, for the favour of the rather pompous gentleman-publisher, who at this time dispensed his patronage among the hungry artists, with an air of conscious superiority. If I am not mistaken in my recollection of the circumstance, this plate was undertaken under the implied condition of " No cure no pay" — that is, if Cooke did not approve, I was to expect nothing. However, I had the good fortune to pass the ordeal of the great man's criticism without being much singed, received six guineas, his average price, and a promise, which was faith-

between us as to what ought to be the price of the plate, I am willing to abide by the decision of any engraver of real respectability that is unconnected with either party.

" I beg to decline the impressions, as I do not wish to receive any obligation that may be considered undeserved.

" I am, Sir,

" Your obedient servant,

" A. RAIMBACH."

[32] Mr. P. Audinet is still living (August, 1836), and resides in the same house in Great Russell Street, Bloomsbury, in which he has resided for more than forty years. He pursues his profession in a quiet, retired, old-fashioned, and independent sort of way. He is unmarried, and, since the death of his uncle (a French Protestant clergyman) and sister with whom he dwelt, his seclusion is complete. Of Mr. Hall's other pupils, I can say but little. Thornthwaite and Reading were the names of two of them, but their works are scarcely known.

fully performed, of future employment. I thus continued to engrave, from time to time, a plate for his editions of the poets and novelists ; I say from time to time, because his publications were not regular, languishing, as did every thing connected with the arts, under the paralysing influence of a war, waged with, perhaps, unprecedented inveteracy. My prospects of success were any thing but encouraging ; but I did not relax in my efforts at improvement. The Mr. Edwards before-mentioned gave me a letter of introduction to the keeper of the Royal Academy, Mr. Wilton,[33] to whom I submitted some specimens of my drawing, and was admitted a probationer forthwith, the facilities of admission being then much greater than at present : I soon after obtained my ticket of student, and in the year 1799 a silver medal for a drawing from the living model. I sedulously pursued my studies at the Royal Academy for about nine years, and am quite ready to acknowledge that I owe much to the opportunities afforded by that establishment. Some few of my studies from the living models were painted in oil. Both the antique and life academies were at this time crowded with young men, aspirants for fame and fortune ; and it is painful to reflect on the very small number, in proportion to the aggregate of students, that have since obtained either the one or the other. And of the few who acquire some celebrity in their day, how rare are the instances of their fame outliving the fortunate possessors themselves ! *Rari nantes in gurgite vasto.* It must be confessed, that, in regard to talent, or even

[33] Wilton, a fine, dignified old gentleman, and a sculptor of some eminence. His bust of Oliver Cromwell has considerable celebrity. His circumstances had become much reduced, from causes that I am unacquainted with ; and the Royal Academicians gave him the keepership, as a refuge in his declining years.

indications of talent, the then actual state of the schools was
little calculated to do honour to the institution ; and so it was
evidently considered by the academicians, inasmuch as an order
of the council was issued, by which it was decreed that every
student in each department (the Antique and the Life) should
submit anew, for the judgment of the academy, a specimen of
his drawing. Some were, in consequence, removed from the
Life to the Antique class, and some from that of the Antique ;
as also those students of ten years standing, who had not obtained a medal, were excluded altogether ; in a way somewhat
analogous to the melancholy process then going on in the nation
at large to a considerable extent, caused by the calamities of
the times, of a remove from the garret to the cellar, and thence
into the street. The effect of this expurgatory ordeal, however,
somewhat exceeded, perhaps, the intentions or expectations of
its framers, as the result was the excitement of a feeling of dis-
gust or mortification among the young men in general, which
led to nearly a desertion of the schools altogether. I distinctly
remember having been more than once the only individual, besides the visiter and the model, in the Life Academy. Mr.
(Sir Martin Archer) Shee was that visiter.

Having passed muster in this harsh and not very judicious
process, I continued my unremitted application to drawing, both
morning and evening attending the library and lectures, and
making the best use in my power of the opportunities for improvement afforded by the academy.

This course of proceeding, though by no means to be regretted, I should not have been able to pursue, but that the
actual state of engraving, still declining from bad to worse, left
me ample leisure to adopt it.

At this time I had occasionally a plate to execute for Cooke's

editions of the poets and novelists, from Kirk,[34] Corbould,[35]
(the elder) Burney,[36] and Thurston,[37] but, like angels' visits,
these commissions were few and far between. This was certainly no very encouraging state of matters, and, under the
circumstances, I turned my attention to painting in miniature ;
at the same time not losing sight of my legitimate profession of
engraving, but with the view of filling up my time, and eking
out an extremely scanty income. I had been accustomed, for
amusement and at " request of friends," to draw the portraits
of my relations and companions, presenting them to the respective individuals ; and, having some facility of execution and
the very common power of making an inveterate likeness, I of
course obtained great credit by my gratuitous performances.
A posthumous miniature-portrait of Stephen Storace, by Arland,[38] which I had engraved for the title-page of the Music of
Mahmoud and the *Iron Chest*, published by his widow, from
having been long under my eye, contributed to forward me in

[34] Kirk had been an engraver and a distinguished student of the Royal
Academy. His designs were small oil-paintings. He died young, of consumption.

[35] Corbould, an ingenious draughtsman and a landscape-painter. His
small drawings for book-decorations are very numerous. His son follows
honourably in the respectable track of his predecessor.

[36] Burney, a nephew of the celebrated Dr. Burney, musician. He was in
considerable vogue at one time, but the *fashion* of his designs did not last.

[37] Thurston was a pupil of Heath, the engraver, but never practised engraving. His drawings were captivating to the eye, from the neatness of
execution, but greatly mannered and incongruous.

[38] Arland was a Swiss, of gentlemanly manners, and painted miniatures
with great taste and beauty of colouring. His likenesses were generally
very good : that of Stephen Storace being a total failure may be easily
accounted for, when it is considered that it was executed almost entirely
from description.

my experiment. I sent some to the exhibition, which I continued to do for several years, and obtained a good many to do at three guineas each. I soon found that I derived great benefit from my attendance at the Royal Academy: not merely from the ordinary studies of the establishment, but for the opportunities afforded by the interchange and collision of ideas with the other young men, and the remarks and occasional conversation of the academicians, chiefly when they officiated as visiters in the Life Academy. Of this number I would especially note Barry,[39] Hamilton,[40] Stothard,[41] Hoppner,[42] Beechey,[43] Northcote,[44]

[39] Barry was uncouth and rough in appearance, but benevolent and gentle in manners towards the young men. In his dispute with the Royal Academy, which terminated in his expulsion, the council, in a manuscript notice placarded in the hall, designated him simply as "James Barry," omitting the "Esquire" at the end of the name, and not even prefixing the ordinary "Mr." This, of course, was meant as a degradation of Barry; but, of the parties contending, it may, I think, fairly admit of a question, whether he was the one degraded by this childish and petulant proceeding.

[40] W. Hamilton, as an artist, now almost forgotten, may be kindly remembered for his amiable and conciliatory character.

[41] Thomas Stothard had great variety of talent, much knowledge, without education, and abundant materials for his art. He was plain, simple, and communicative, and may certainly be considered one of the ornaments of his profession.

[42] James Hoppner — an admirable portrait-painter, haughty in manner, and satirical and bitter in his conversation, as well as in his reviews in the *Quarterly*, of the editor of which he was the friend and constant companion. Hoppner was said to have royal blood flowing in his veins.

[43] Sir W. Beechey—respectable talents, aided by great good-fortune—vulgar manners, with considerable shrewdness.

[44] James Northcote — distinguished both in art and literature — cynical and parsimonious in his personal character; yet friendly and encouraging to the juniors — of low stature, and had a good deal of the look of an old-clothes-man, but with marked features, and an eye like a hawk.

Opie,[45] Tresham,[46] Shee, Fuseli,[47] Banks,[48] Nollekens,[49] and Flaxman.[50] Some of them occasionally made studies from the model during their visitation : Hamilton in particular was as assiduous as a novice ; and his drawings displayed great

[45] John Opie was naturally of somewhat coarse and blunt demeanour, but I think he affected to be more so. He was very popular in his day, but that day was a short one. He died at an early age, yet had outlived his celebrity. Northcote and Opie were in a manner considered rivals, and the works of both are now nearly, if not quite, forgotten.

[46] Henry Tresham — a native of Ireland, and another instance of varied talents unsuccessful. Here was a painter, poet, lecturer, and gentleman, utterly neglected. In early life he had passed some years in Italy, and was intimate with Canova. He was of debilitated health ; though in 1803, when threats of invasion called the whole nation to arms, Tresham was a member of the committee of artists, who assembled to form a volunteer corps. It was observed, on seeing his name at the head of the list, "that, when the peaceful arts themselves took the field, led on by Thresh'em, the great Bonaparte would surely pause in his attempt."

[47] Henry Fuseli—a man of undoubted genius, though, as a painter, his claims to pre-eminence may be disputed—an excellent Greek scholar, with extensive acquirements in various departments of literature. His knowledge and command of our language contrasted strongly with his foreign pronunciation. He was a native of Zurich; in person of small stature, with a large head, and grey hair flowing like a lion's mane, and proud and polished in his demeanour.

[48] Banks. [49] Nollekens. [50] Flaxman. The three great English sculptors of their time. We may refer in proof of this assertion to the " Achilles," the "Caractacus," the "Mahratta Chieftain " of Banks, in Sir Eyre Coote's monument : to the monuments of " Mrs. Howard of Corby," of " the three Captains," in Westminster Abbey, and numerous busts of Nollekens : and the various works of Flaxman, both in design and sculpture. Nollekens was one of those anomalies of nature, which are occasionally to be met with in every pursuit, and which may in his instance be characterized by a parody of Garrick's epitaph on Goldsmith :—

" *He sculptured like Phidias,* and talked like poor Poll !"

elegance, though they were not very faithful to nature. Barry's had a rough grandeur of style, and were executed with the commonest materials ; usually on a fragment of coarse paper, with the pen and ink, which served the young men to write their names in the hall as they arrived. Stothard made slight and small sketches, that were replete with character and action. Flaxman's drawings from the academy figure were highly-wrought pure imitations of nature, viewed through the medium of his refined, antique, and cultivated mind.

To resume my narrative. My miniature-painting commissions increasing, and those for engraving certainly not relaxing, I soon found that it would be necessary to decide upon giving up the one or the other as a profession. Though it may not be in accordance with the proverb, " Two strings to your bow," it is, I believe, generally admitted that one trade, well learned and steadily pursued, is better than two less known and irregularly followed. I did not, however, in my final determination in this momentous concern, act solely on my own judgment, but took the opinions of others whose judgment and experience were entitled to respect and consideration. The taste I had had of the business of portrait-painting, though it was but in a small way, most assuredly did not enchant me. The purchaser of an article, be it what it may, feels a right, in laying out his money, to have the commodity he pays for suited to his liking, if it be possible. Now, taste is so capricious, and personal vanity so difficult to satisfy, that it is no wonder that the self-respect and feelings of independence which, I presume, every man possesses in a greater or lesser degree, are liable to great mortification in the profession of portrait-painting. I, certainly, in my very humble efforts, found it so, and I am greatly mistaken if much abler men have not found it so too. Engraving, whatever

may be its disadvantages, (and they are many) has not the
fancies of individuals to humour or consult, but appeals at once
to the public, or to that small part of the public that takes an
interest in such trivialities. The opinions I had solicited con-
curred with my own feelings on the subject ; and, thus fortified,
I did not hesitate to adopt the course I have since unremittingly
pursued, namely, to devote my whole attention to engraving.
Looking back at past events, I do not know that I have any
reason to regret the decision I then came to.

About four years passed away in this manner without any
material change of circumstances, I continuing to engrave small
plates when I could obtain them for the *Poets*, *Novels*, *German
Theatre*, &c., and devoting the large remainder of time almost
exclusively to academical studies, in the hope of more propitious opportunity, and of better qualifying myself to profit by a
favourable change, if it should arrive. Though my attendance
at the academy was very regular, I must not be understood as
having no inclination for or participation in the current amusements of the day, like other young men of my own standing.
The theatres had always been a source of great enjoyment to
me ; and the connection of Mr. Hall with theatrical persons, by
the marriage of his daughter with Storace, not only afforded
me the opportunity of seeing some of them at his table, but led
also to my receiving many gratuitous admissions to their performances during my pupilage. Subsequently, I had a still
greater advantage of the same kind, from an acquaintance with
the people of the *Morning Post* newspaper,[51] by whose means I

---

[51] Daniel Stuar·, the editor and chief proprietor of the *Morning Post*
at that time, and afterwards of the *Courier*, had a very humble beginning,
having been, as I was informed, originally a journeyman tailor. He had a
brother, (Peter) likewise a newspaper editor, though I forget the name of

could often avail myself of free admission to one or other of the places of public entertainment, though I seldom or never went, during the session at Somerset House, till the close of the schools at eight o'clock. I must, however, admit that my presence at the playhouses was not always (though it was most frequently) quite unconditional, being sometimes requested, in the absence of the regular reporter, to supply the theatrical critique. I was ready-handed enough in such matters, and found too much pleasure in this commission to feel either constraint or embarrassment in its execution; and I can most truly declare (what few critics by profession are able to do) that I was rather disposed to commend than to censure, and that censure itself, as administered by me, was not of that caustic quality that characterizes the effusions of our modern Aristarchuses. In fact, it came to my knowledge that, on more than one occasion, my observations had given great pleasure to the subjects of them, (a somewhat rare occurrence, I believe) who had even expressed a desire to be acquainted with the writer of them. One of these actors, an eminent man, is now (1836) living; many others are gone to their long home; and, though my vanity might have been gratified by the avowal of these and many other scribblings, it was so much under control of my pride that the incognito was never discovered, however much suspicion may have been raised. I may be allowed to mention here that I

his journal. They were both clever men, and connected, by the marriage of a sister, with Sir James Mackintosh. Daniel made a fortune rapidly, and is, I believe, still living (1836) at Brompton Park. He was accused of forging a copy of *L'Eclair*, a French paper, for stock-jobbing purposes. James Nott made a handsome property as publisher of the *Morning Post*. He had been a hair-dresser, " whose harvest was spoiled," according to the phrase of the day, " by too many crops."

had shown rather early a certain degree of facility in stringing
sentences together, as, at the age of fourteen, I found, much to
my surprise, two of my lucubrations in print. They appeared
in different numbers of Ayres's *Sunday Gazette*,[52] a newspaper
published in Brydges Street, Covent Garden, and were critical,
ironical, and artistical. The office had no letter-box in the window,
and, being ashamed to deliver them to the clerk, I threw them
at dark down the area, with little expectation as to the result.
They were read and *highly admired* by some of my acquaintance ;
but I was of course never suspected, and to *this moment* I have
kept the mighty secret. At a later period, contributions of
mine, both in verse and prose, have found their way into print,
but always unavowed.   The reason, valid or not, as it may be,
for this shyness on my part, can be explained in a few words.
When a certain degree of credit has been acquired by legitimate
means in a profession, any efforts not successful in another track
never fail to have the effect, however unjustly, of impairing
the previously-obtained reputation, more or less, according to
the degree of failure in the newly-attempted province ; and, as
I most surely did not estimate my *nugæ literariæ* very highly,
and had at the same time some hopes of establishing myself as
an artist, it will not be wondered at that I chose to " shoot my
blunt arrows from behind a bush."
　　At the latter end of the year 1801, a publication was projected, which is entitled to notice, inasmuch as it was the first
of a series that tended greatly to elevate the character of decorated books : the work chosen in the present instance was the
Arabian Nights' Entertainments, to be embellished with twenty-

[52] This was one of the very few Sunday papers that were published
about that time (1790). It has long ceased to exist.

four engravings from pictures by Smirke.[53] The projector was
the Rev. Edward Forster,[54] a person who afterwards became
well known among the artists by his various speculations ; and
associated with him was Miller, the bookseller, the predecessor
of Murray, in Albemarle Street. Forster was to supply a new
translation from the French of M. Galland. The engravers se-

[53] Robert Smirke is a name that may not be passed over by me without
a tribute of respect and acknowledgment for advantages obtained in the
repeated communications I necessarily had with him, professionally. Mr.
Smirke is, I believe, a native of Cumberland, and was born about the
year 1760. At an early age he was apprenticed to a coach-herald painter,
and his detractors were accustomed to say that his pictures looked like
coach-panels. Almost all artists in their outset have to struggle with indigence, as well as obscurity, and Smirke was no exception to the general
rule. On the contrary, his probation was perhaps longer than ordinary ;
and, till Boydell's great enterprise afforded him a favourable opportunity
of showing of what he was capable, his chief or only occupation was
making small designs for the *Novelist's Magazine*, &c., as Stothard had
done before him. Those who remember the *Shakspere Gallery* will
bear testimony to the admirable talent displayed in Smirke's pictures,
wherein, with subjects greatly varied, he proved himself a master equally
of pathos, humour, beauty, grace, and dignity : while, in regard to execution, the drawing, colouring, composition, and effect, left scarcely any thing
to be desired. He is still living, (1836) but has long ceased to exercise his
art. He is author of two satires, *Midas*, and the *Catalogue Raisonné* of
the British Institution.
[54] The Rev. Edward Forster, M.A., F.R.S., a clergyman of the established church, Lecturer at the Royal Institution, preacher at various
chapels, and editor of various works, viz : — The British Gallery of Engravings, The British Theatre, &c. &c. He married Banks the sculptor's
daughter, an accomplished woman, and, after a short and bustling career
in London, suddenly disappeared, and I believe was not seen again in England. He was much addicted to card-playing, and afterwards turned up
in France as chaplain to the British Embassy ; but his creditors never
obtained anything. He used to preach at the Oratoire in Paris.

lected were Heath, Fittler,[55] Anker Smith,[56] Neagle,[57] Parker,[58] Warren,[59] Armstrong,[60] and myself.

[55] James Fittler, an artist of respectable talent, great industry, and considerable reputation at one time. He engraved several large plates of the Naval Victories after Loutherbourg. Fittler resided many years in Charlotte Street, in good style, keeping a servant in livery (as also did Sharpe in the meridian of his career.) He died in 1835, aged about 70, in impoverished circumstances at Turnham Green, where he had lived in retirement for the latter part of his life, surviving both fortune and popularity.

[56] Anker Smith's reputation was scarcely equal to his merit as an artist. He wrought most diligently for the booksellers, by whom he was chiefly employed. His Death of Wat Tyler, a large plate, was not a successful work, and a still larger one, The Duke of Wellington and his Officers, was left unfinished at his death, and led to tedious and expensive litigation between his widow and Heaphy, the designer. Anker Smith died suddenly, aged about sixty-three.

[57] James Neagle, an Irishman, and an engraver of most promising abilities, which seemed unfortunately to decline gradually as he grew older. He emigrated to the United States.

[58] James Parker, a fellow pupil of the insane genius Blake, at Basire's—not very distinguished as an artist, but greatly respected for his amiable disposition, integrity, and good sense. He died after a short illness, aged about forty-five.

[59] Charles Warren. Many of this artist's book-plates are of the most exquisite beauty of execution. He was very desirous of engraving a large plate, that, as he said, he might have something that would show what he could do; but though he planned and talked of several schemes for the purpose, he did not accomplish it. He was a well-meaning man, of a friendly disposition, an agreeable companion, and fond of jovial society, for which he was well adapted by his perfect self-confidence, his talent for singing, and his power of making a speech: qualities which perhaps were rather injurious than beneficial to him. He died quite suddenly while employed at his work-table, aged about fifty-three.

[60] Cosmo Armstrong, with much power of execution, has been too irregular in his application and too eccentric in character to take the rank in his profession that he might otherwise have done. He is still living, I believe (1836).

I have already stated that a Society of Engravers was formed at the time of the trial between Copley and Delattre. The intentions of this society were, first, by publishing their own works, to receive the whole profit ; and secondly, the establishment of a benevolent fund for the relief of their distressed brethren and their families. The scheme was not successful ; but, since that attempt, these objects have been effected by other associations. The engravers engaged in the *Arabian Nights* becoming, through their co-operation in that work, better acquainted with each other, were accustomed to meet monthly at each other's residences, as a social club. This meeting was not only very agreeable in itself, but also greatly serviceable to the members of it professionally. Their union gave the means of enabling each individual to act with more firmness in opposing the pretensions of those who had been considered, justly or not, their natural oppressors—the booksellers and publishers. The mutual jealousy of men engaged in the same pursuits is then merged, by the *esprit de corps*, into a common feeling of resistance to their (supposed) tyrannical employers. I could name more than one instance where this principle was acted upon by individuals of this union with results highly favourable to the immediate interests of the combinators.

About this time, (1802) I was lodging in Charles Street, at the house of a French modeller named Chenu, where I had opportunities, which I did not neglect, of studying from some excellent casts from the antique, and of improving an already tolerable acquaintance with the French language, by frequent conversation. The short-lived peace that had just been patched up between England and France opened the route to the continent, which had been closed for ten or twelve years, and the eager curiosity of Englishmen to visit the scenes of revolutionary horrors and eventful changes that had taken place in the interim greatly added to the ordinary interest of a journey to Paris; which, by the by, was then in itself a much more serious undertaking than a similar excursion at present, rendered as it is so rapid and pleasurable by steamboats and safety-coaches. It would be difficult to convey an idea of the *rush* that was made to the French capital by persons of every class who had the means of transit in their power. The artists in particular mustered in much greater force on this occasion than could have been anticipated, taking into account the proverbial scantiness of their resources. As soon as I had completed my three plates for the *Arabian Nights*, and had received payment for them, (a *sine quâ non* in regard to my expedition) I lost no time in putting into execution the plan I had for some time entertained of passing a week or two, or three, according to circumstances, in the then centre of general attraction. In consequence, having provided myself with a passport from Lord Hawkesbury's office,[61] I set out on the morning of Thursday, the 8th of July, 1802, for Paris, by Brighton and Dieppe. The fare to Brighton was then, owing to a strong opposition, but half a guinea inside. It is now thirty-four years since I saw this famous watering-place, and then only for a day, but I have still a pretty distinct recollection of it as it was,

---

[61] Passports at that time might be obtained from the French *chargé d'affaires* without any expense, while those delivered from the English secretary of state's office were saddled with the payment of £2 5s. each, besides the necessity of some formal recommendation. It was, however, thought to be most prudent, in the then feverish state of public feeling between France and England, to be provided with that which authorized the bearer to claim the protection of the British ambassador in any political emergency.

though I am told that I should now have some difficulty in recognizing those parts I formerly knew, so great have been the changes.

I embarked with twenty-five other passengers from off Brighton, on the 9th, and, after a very rough passage, in which I and most of the people on board were drenched to the skin, by the sea washing over the little vessel, arrived at Dieppe at five in the morning of the 10th, landing on French ground in a glorious sunrise and calm that was quite delicious after the gale of the preceding day. I have never at any time since been so much struck with the novelty and strangeness of a scene as that which Dieppe presented. Its effect on me was no doubt increased by the circumstance of my never having quitted England before: though I think, notwithstanding, that Dieppe has in itself, its population, manners, and costume, much more to surprise and interest a foreign visiter than the usual *ports d'entrée* of Calais or Boulogne. Having comparatively but little intercourse with England, Dieppe retains its national characteristics in all their freshness and vigour, and formed at that time a most striking contrast to the country I had just quitted. The rude, insolent, revolutionary manners of the people in general; the *sans-culottism* of the male, and the tall Norman cap and long-ear pendants of the female costume; the great number and irrepressible importunity of beggars of all ages; the dragging of loaded carts, and the carriage of heavy burthens by women; and the coarseness, filth, and slovenliness of domestic habits, constituted the materials of a living picture that no lapse of years will efface from my memory.

I remained but half a day at Dieppe, having taken breakfast and an early, excellent, and very cheap dinner, (in which the turbot was pre-eminent) at the Hôtel d'Angleterre, setting out for Rouen immediately afterwards in an old, ragged, rickety machine, of the covered cabriolet kind, carrying three passengers, and drawn by two rough and poor-looking horses of different sizes, the smallest of which was the subject of continual commendation from the postillion, a man about fifty years old. Indeed, the animal fully justified, by his endurance, the praises of his master, as we made the journey almost without a pause, though our cattle had only that morning travelled the distance from Rouen to Dieppe, and had since rested but about six hours. Our pace was slow,[62] and we reached Rouen about eleven at night, finding the town silent, still, and dark.

On entering the folding gates of an hotel to which we had been recommended by our host at Dieppe, a few glimmering lights were seen in the lower part of the house, and after a slight and hasty repast, I was conducted across a large courtyard to my quarters for the night, an immense room whose gloom and extent my candle could not illuminate, and in a remote corner of which stood a bed. In this gigantic temple of solitary repose was I left to my meditations, and I confess that they were not altogether free from uneasy fancies. However, no brigand disturbed this my first night's rest in France, and I was awakened after a sound and refreshing sleep by the cheerful rays of a bright sun darting on my pillow, and with the unromantic feeling of an eager appetite for breakfast. This morning (11th July) being Sunday, I entered the magnificent Cathedral, and witnessed the performance of mass, and afterwards strolled about the town and suburbs. The city of

[62] The Norman nags do not make a handsome appearance, but are capable of great and long-continued exertion. It was proved, during the war, that they bore the wear and tear of a campaign better than our large and handsome half-bred horses.

Rouen is large and irregularly built ; the churches [63] numerous, and the streets very narrow. The bridge of boats across the river interests the curiosity of strangers, and the environs and views from the heights above the town are beautiful beyond description. The populace here appeared under circumstances even more unfavourable than usual. There was a supposed scarcity of bread, and the people were clamorous and violent, assembling in crowds about the bakers' shops ; but a mere demonstration of military force, by parading the dragoons with drawn sabres through the streets, was found sufficient to quiet the tumult, without the necessity of resorting to extreme measures. Bread was at this time four sous a pound, (it had been as high as six) while, under the old *régime*, two and a half was the ordinary price. The French are highly susceptible and soon excited on this subject, inasmuch as bread forms a more than common proportion of their food. In the evening I went to the play, and found the house crammed from top to bottom, with an audience of a somewhat coarse description, Sunday being in France the most popular and least select night for the theatres. As I went rather late, I saw only part of a *pièce de spectacle*, which had nothing either in it or its actors that need be noticed. The *salle* was spacious and handsome, but very dirty and much in want of repair.

Being anxious to reach Paris for the *fête* of the 14th of July, (the anniversary celebration of the destruction of the Bastille) I was a good deal put out by the difficulty, or what rather seemed then like the impossibility of procuring a place in any vehicle, in sufficient time for the show, seeing that so many

[63] The church of St. Maclou remarkable for the lightness and elegance of its tower.

others were striving to accomplish the same object.   Aided in
my efforts by a friendly fellow-traveller from Dieppe (a Frenchman) who had business at Rouen, and knew the place well, I
tried every feasible quarter without success, and had indeed
given up all hopes, when, at the suggestion of my French
friend, another application was made in private to the *conducteur*
of one of the diligences, and assisted as it was by a judicious administration of a certain efficacious material to the palm of the
hand, our urgent solicitations were at length crowned with success, and I was to be allowed to mount the *impériale* as a super-
numerary passenger.   I passed another night in my capacious
dormitory, and at four o'clock in the morning (12th of July)
took my allotted station on the roof of the diligence, which in
those days was quite unprovided with any shelter from the weather, and found myself one of a mixed company that certainly
exceeded the lawful number.   This was especially our *conducteur's* affair, and he seemed to manage it with all the skill of an
experienced hand, by directing occasional gettings-down of some
of the upper passengers as we approached particular places, and
gettings-up again after they were passed.   The weather was
serene and clear, and the effects of the great heat, to which, as
the day advanced, we of the upper surface were exposed, was
I think, a good deal mitigated by the lightness and purity of
the air.   Whether it was so or not, I am at least quite sure
that in England I have often felt myself much more oppressed
by a lower degree of temperature.   The distance from Rouen
to the capital is about ninety miles, and the road lies through a
fertile and beautiful country, luxuriant in vegetation and rich
in flocks and herds, delightful to the sight, and strongly contrasting by its varied and picturesque scenery with the level,
monotonous province of Picardy—the route most frequented by

Englishmen. The road itself improves as you approach the metropolis ; and, passing Pontoise, a town situated, as its name indicates, on the banks of the river, and famous for calves and millers, and afterwards through St. Denis, still more famous for its venerable abbey, the magnificent cemetery of monarchs, we arrived about seven o'clock in the evening at Paris.

Among the many points of difference between England and France, in national habits, may be reckoned that of the French being essentially an out-of-door people. The domestic fireside does not seem to have the same attaching qualities that constitute the greatest charm of existence in England. This out-of-door habit prevails with the French at all seasons ; and therefore it is no wonder that, on my entrance into Paris, at the close of a hot summer's day, I should have erroneously estimated its population at much more than the actual number. On the Boulevards, a full tide of human beings flowed on in a continued stream, fluttering in all the gay colours of the rainbow, and harmonised and softened by the glowing tints of the setting sun. All the main streets through which we passed in our way to the Messageries presented the appearance of large assemblies just broken up, while those persons whom occupation or circumstances compelled to remain at home indulged the natural propensity, as far as it was possible, by seating themselves on chairs and benches placed outside their houses. The whole scene was most animating and agreeable ; but there was a little drawback on its otherwise unqualified interest, in the peculiar odour that forces itself upon the attention of a stranger : it arises partly from the French cookery, and partly, I should think, from the practice of casting into the streets the refuse of the kitchen, decaying vegetables, &c., and cannot be entirely got rid of either by the labour of the scavengers, or by the supple-

mental exertions of the kennel-rakers (*chiffoniers*). As I am
constitutionally rather susceptible in my olfactories, and " ab-
hor evil smells " as sincerely as did Queen Elizabeth herself,
I was not able at first to reconcile myself to Paris on this score ;
but, after a few days' residence, the annoyance is no longer noticed. I took up my quarters at the Hôtel Mont Orgueil, Rue
Mont Orgueil, a large establishment of two hundred rooms, in
the sixth story of which I occupied a very comfortable bed-
room. The street, rather a mean one, has the honour of being
the birthplace of the celebrated *chansonnier*, Béranger.

On the morning after my arrival, (13th July) I started be-
times to seek a person whose address had been very inaccu-
rately given me. In the course of my search, although I had
ascertained that I was in the right track, it was still necessary
to make some inquiries. For this purpose I accosted a decent,
tradesman-like man, whose aspect pleased me, and who was
proceeding at a quick pace, evidently on business. He came
to a full stop, listened attentively to what I had to state, and
then, saying that he thought he could show me the place I was
looking for, turned his steps in a different direction to that in
which he was previously going, and, after some intricate wind-
ings, pointed out, with much kindness of manner, the very
house I wanted to find. At parting, I of course was desirous
of making my acknowledgments, in the best French I could
muster, for the service he had rendered me, when he cut short
my speech by expressing his conviction that, in similar circumstances, he, or any stranger, would have met with the same
civility in England. I did not by any means feel so sure of
that ; though I took special care not to lessen the good opinion
he professed towards my countrymen. I mention this trivial
incident, in justice to that kind and attentive politeness which

every one that has passed some time among the French must, more or less, have experienced, and which, under every change, has, I believe, shown itself as identified with their national cha- racter : nor do I see that we have any right very scrupulously to question the motive, be it vanity or good-will, which prompts a conduct that manifests at least a disposition to honour their country, and contributes, as all must admit, very largely to the enjoyment of their visiters.

As the day of the grand *fête* approached, "the busy note of preparation" was heard on all sides : the palaces and public buildings were destined for illumination ; the bridge of the Pont Neuf for fireworks ; and the Place Vendôme and Champs Elysées for dancing, *mats de cocagne*, and distribution of pro- visions : reviews of troops and court-receptions for the morning ; gratuitous representations at the theatres and concerts in the open air, in the Tuileries gardens, for the evening. Paris was crowded with visiters from the provinces and with strangers from all countries : among the latter, our countrymen mustered in great force. Every thing went on favourably ; and, to crown all, the weather (July 14th) was propitious.

The most distinguishing feature of a holiday festival in France, as far as my opportunities have enabled me to form an opinion, is the hilarity and abandonment to the impulse of en- joyment, which seem universally to prevail on such occasions among this lively and happy-tempered people. Every eye beamed with cheerfulness, and sounds of mirth and good-humour met the ear in all directions. Indeed, the animated expression of the populace and their gay yet orderly demeanour formed by far the chief interest of the scene to a looker-on. The *fête* itself did not by any means equal my expectations : the fireworks on the bridge would not go off ; the concert in the garden could

not be heard ; and the illuminations, though in good taste, were
not sufficiently general to mark a decided national feeling.   I
returned to my hotel at a late hour, a good deal amused, and
not a little fatigued with the day's entertainment.   During my
stay in Paris, I witnessed another celebration of a similar kind,
on the occasion of Bonaparte's inauguration as First Consul for
life.   It differed scarcely at all from the preceding, with perhaps the exception of a more evident ebullition of popular sentiment in favour of its idol ; one part at least of whose policy
seemed, like that of the old Roman republic, soothing the people
with *panem et circenses*.   After all, none of the *fétes* that I ever
witnessed, either at this visit to Paris or subsequently, were
to be compared with those I have seen in England, which,
though "few and far between," make up by their amplitude
and magnificence for the infrequency of their occurrence.   I
would name, as of my own recollection, those of the Jubilee, in
the 50th year of George the Third's reign, and the coronation
of George the Fourth.   The variety and profusion of the one
and the splendour of the other were doubtless the result of superior powers and more extended resources.

One of the greatest and best appreciated attractions of Paris
at this epoch was the unequalled assemblage of antique statues
and pictures by the old masters, the plunder of conquered
countries ; or, as the French had inscribed on the cornice,
Les fruits de nos victoires !   It would be impossible to convey
in words an adequate idea of the grand and solemn effect produced by those marvellous works of ages past, which were
gratuitously exhibited to public view in the noble halls and
galleries of the Louvre.   Strangers in particular had much
reason to be gratified by the extraordinary facilities of viewing
these wonders so liberally afforded them, on the mere showing

of their passports, and even on days when the inhabitants themselves were not admitted : a preference that never excited a murmur among the Parisians. I had obtained without difficulty, as an artist, a *carte d'entrée*, which gave me the privilege of admission, for the purpose of drawing, early in the mornings, several hours before the admission of the public. Of this privilege I availed myself every day, making studies from the original Torso, Laocoon, &c. The Apollo Belvidere was the most attractive object of the collection, riveting the admiration of every beholder, while the Venus de Medicis, long expected, arrived at last, and took her station in this glorious assemblage as the *ne plus ultra* of beauty, grace, and symmetry.

On ascending the staircase, in itself unrivalled for elegance of construction, you enter the spacious saloon ; at that time mainly appropriated to the grand productions of the Venetian school. Here burst upon the astonished sight the gorgeous work (still remaining there) of Paolo Veronese, the Marriage of Cana ; together with the St. Georgio, by the same great artist ; the Pietro Martire of Titian ; the Conversion of St. Mark, by Tintoretto. In this division was also to be seen, among many pictures of the highest class, Vandyke's whole length of Cardinal Bentivoglio—the very perfection of portrait-painting, and forming part, I believe, of the royal collection of France. The extent of French spoliation, great as it was, has, however, been much exaggerated, and a very large proportion of the choicest specimens of the art had been collected by Francis I., Louis XIV., and other monarchs who, either from taste or ostentation, were munificent in their patronage of artists. The gallery, nearly a quarter of a mile long, issuing from the saloon, covered on both sides its whole length with pictures, very many of them masterpieces of their respective schools, was an inexhaustible fund of study and enjoyment. It would be a vain effort on my part to enter into a detailed account, or even to attempt a regular enumeration of the most striking *chefs-d'œuvre*. As the best descriptions of works of art, if not altogether useless, are found to give but a very inadequate idea to the reader of the subjects treated on, I shall not attempt to do more than mention a few of those that made the most lasting impression on my memory. Of all that the collection contained, the greatest sensation was produced on the public by the numerous Rubens's, clustered as they were in a mass, and of very large dimensions. Their grandeur of composition, brilliancy of colouring, and force of effect, eclipsing every thing around them, irresistibly arrested the attention. Most of these have, by the course of events, been restored to their former situations, and I have since seen some of the finest of them in the cathedral at Antwerp. The magical results of Rembrandt's exquisite management of the *chiar' oscuro*, the perfect harmony of tone, and the bold originality of his mode of treating his subjects, were never more vividly displayed than in the pictures here exhibited. Vandyke, also, together with Ostade, Teniers, Brouwer, Gerard Douw, Netscher, Cuyp, Hobbima, and Ruysdael, contributed their full share to the glories of the Dutch and Flemish schools. But the Italian pictures! What pen could do justice to the sublime, the transcendent excellence of this department of the gallery! I shall confine myself to the mere enumeration of a few only of the most memorable objects. The Transfiguration of Raphael; [64]

[64] The Transfiguration was not at this time actually in the Gallery. It was in a private apartment, undergoing some process at the hands of a French restorer of pictures; but, in the temporary absence of the operator, by a timely gratuity to one of the attendants, I obtained admittance.

the Marriage of St. Catherine, by Correggio ;[65] the Communion of St. Jerome,[66] and Martyrdom of St. Agnes, by Domenichino; our Saviour and the Doctors of the Church, by Leonardo da Vinci ; the Entombment of Christ, by Titian. The four first named, each of which would dignify any national collection in Europe, are no longer in the keeping of our Gallic neighbours, but, with numbers of others by the Caracci, Guido, Albano, Guercino, and others, have been removed to their original stations. Notwithstanding the searching measure of retribution that has been imposed on them, they may still boast of possessing many of the finest works of art in existence, as the present display in the Louvre amply testifies. The old French school of painting, though not to be ranked as equal to the highest, has in itself much that is entitled to respectful and attentive consideration. The names of Poussin and Claude stand at the very head of their respective departments : in philosophic history and in landscape what can be named in competition with the works of these two great artists?—while those of Lebrun, Le Sueur, Mignard, Gaspar Poussin, Vernet, and Greuze, contain excellencies that may be studied with great advantage.

The Louvre, as may be readily supposed, was the grand centre of attraction to the English in Paris, more especially to the artists. Among the more distinguished visiters was Mr. Fox, whom I also saw at the Opera and at Frescati. He

[65] Of this splendid work of Correggio, which throws to an immeasurable distance all that bears his name in England that I have ever seen, it was said that Bonaparte had been offered a very large sum of money in lieu of it by the authorities of Parma, whence the picture came. But this story was thought to be discredited by the probability that, in such a case, the triumphant soldier would have taken both.

[66] This famous picture has been considered as second only to the Transfiguration of Raphael.

was accompanied by Mrs. Fox and Lord Holland, and some other gentlemen. It was highly gratifying to witness the excitement caused among the Frenchmen by his presence, and scarcely less so to perceive with what delicacy of tact they managed to indulge an ardent curiosity towards the illustrious man, without even the slightest approach to rudeness or vulgarity, or what might in any way interfere with his enjoyment of the scene before him.

Of the English artists at that time in Paris I could give rather a long list, but I shall confine myself to the mention of only a few : West,[67] Turner,[68] Phillips,[69] Opie, Thomas

[67] Benjamin West is well known by the biographies of Galt and others. It is melancholy to reflect on the almost total oblivion into which his works have now fallen. Surely there must be at some future time a revival of them, or we shall, as a nation, in a measure justify the libellous imputation of being incapable of appreciating the higher productions of art. It must be admitted that West's *talk* did not contribute any aid to his talents as an artist, but rather the contrary. His everlasting subject, himself, paraded with all the garrulity of old age, and abundantly adorned with those figures of speech designated slip-slop twaddle and rigmarole, was equally out of keeping both with his works and with the shrewd and intelligent expression of his countenance.

[68] William Turner — a genius of the highest order, and not the less so for his occasionally soaring beyond the reach of sober judgment. He stayed but a short time in Paris, where his residence became irksome, partly from his want of acquaintance with the language perhaps, and partly from the paucity of materials afforded to his peculiar studies. He very soon directed his steps to the south of France and Italy. This great artist's works are among the few that will take a distinguished rank in times to come. He was born in London, and is the son of a decent tradesman, who carried on a small business in Maiden Lane, Covent Garden ; and it is to his son's credit that the old man's declining years were soothed by filial attention, and passed in comfort and repose.

[69] Thomas Phillips is, I believe, a native of Birmingham, and, unlike the

Daniell,[70] Shee, and Flaxman. Mr. West brought with him
and exhibited in the *Exposition au Salon* his well-known and
justly celebrated picture, [finished sketch] " Death on the pale
Horse," from the Apocalypse. It was greatly admired, and
the painter highly complimented by all ranks—the first Consul
himself shewing him marked attention. Among other distinctions he was invited to a festival by the artists, at which old
Vien, the then *Doyen* of the Academy, delivered an oration
in the highest style of French hyperbole. It is not to be
wondered at that West's mind was intoxicated by such adulation, and that his " more than female vanity," as I have heard
it designated by one of his most eminent contemporaries,
should have displayed itself with characteristic simplicity.
This has been well depicted in the anecdote introduced by
Allan Cunningham, in his clever Biographies of the Painters :
" Wherever I went," said West, " people looked at me, and
ministers and men of influence in the state were constantly in
my company. I was one day in the Louvre — all eyes were
upon me, and I could not help observing to Charles Fox, *who*

subject of the preceding note, is any thing but a man of genius; but, by dint
of study and persevering industry, combined with good sense and good
conduct, has succeeded so far as to place himself in the very first rank of
portrait-painters of the present day. Indeed, after Lawrence, Owen, and
Jackson, I hardly know any one entitled to take precedence of Phillips in
his peculiar department. This gentleman's successful career may be re-
ferred to as an encouragement to the student, as the result of average
ability, cultivated with unremitting application. His early efforts were
very unpromising. His Lectures are, of course, a transcript of his mind :
they command respect, but elicit no admiration.

70 Thomas Daniell is known only by his Views in India. He has from
age and infirmity long discontinued the practice of his art, (1836) but his
nephew, William Daniell, more than supplies his place.

happened to be walking with me, how strong was the love of Art and admiration of its professors in France ! ! "

As I made it a point of duty to avail myself of every opportunity of drawing from the ancient statues, I became thereby somewhat acquainted with some of the young French artists who were studying in the magnificent " Hall of Antiques." Among others was Horace Vernet, the present celebrated painter, then a lively boy of thirteen or fourteen years old.   I was introduced also to his father, Carle Vernet,[71] Isabey,[72]

---

[71] Artistical talent is hereditary in the family of Vernet.   Three generations have made their name and works familiar to all the cognoscenti of Europe.   The marine pieces of the first of the name, although eclipsed by those of our own school, are still entitled to respectful consideration. Carle Vernet is best known by his hunting and battle subjects, in which his thorough acquaintance with the anatomical structure of the horse and dog is abundantly displayed.   His temper was cheerful, and his manners were gay—not to say juvenile—to a very advanced age.   He was a member of the Institute, and died in Paris, December, 1836, aged about 80 years. Horace Vernet, his son, is perhaps the ablest artist of this highly-gifted stock.   He is no less distinguished by the excellence than by the versatility of his talents.   On the death of M. Guérin, Horace was appointed by the Institute (of which he is also a member), Director of the French Academy at Rome, an establishment that has for many years been maintained at a very considerable expense, and has enjoyed a rather high reputation.   It would appear, however, that Vernet formed a less favourable judgment of the benefit to be derived from it, having, it is said, on his return to Paris, recommended its suppression.   Horace Vernet is now (1836) at St. Petersburgh, at the invitation of the Emperor Nicholas, who received him with honours and distinctions unprecedented in the annals of art.

[72] Isabey — the miniature-painter of the government, and rather a favourite of the First Consul; an artist of great power in his peculiar province, and possessing some imagination, which found a field of operation congenial to its degree in the decorations (as the French term the scenery) of the Opera House.   Some of his designs for this purpose, with others of

Bervic,[73] and others. At that time they resided in apartments
adjoining the Louvre, and I believe were allowed besides a small
pension from government. These privileges no longer exist in
that form, but are merged in those attached to members of the In-

various kinds, besides miniatures, were exhibited by him in Pall Mall about
the year 1814. His son, a young man of great promise, studied a good deal
in England, and has produced some admirable sea-shore views somewhat
in the style of our Collins.

[73] Bervic, the engraver, was a pupil of Wille, and combined with a
nearly similar command of mechanical ability some approaches to excellence
in higher qualities of art. His known and celebrated works are of elaborate
perfection of execution, and, as far as I recollect, do not exceed half a
dozen in number. The large portrait of Louis XVI., after a very indifferent
picture by Callet, is a fine specimen of Bervic's powers; the head itself,
perhaps, being the least successful part of it. The Centaur carrying away
Dejanira, after the picture by Guido; the Education of Achilles, after
Regnault, and the Laocoon, from the antique; and Fidelity, from a picture
by Merimée, are all that I can enumerate. He was of a manly, independent temper of mind, that made itself not only generally respected, but, as
I have been given to understand, more particularly in the Institute, of
which he had been a member from its first establishment by the Republican
government, in 1794-1795. The name Bervic (Berwick?) would indicate
a British origin, and I should willingly flatter my own nationality with the
idea that his frank, candid, and liberal manners might in some way be re-
ferred to England. I was greatly pleased by his reception of me, and
had occasion to communicate with him by letter two or three times afterwards. His pupil, Henriquel Dupont, worthily sustains the reputation of
his school. He died in 1822. I should have mentioned that his plate of
Louis XVI. was destroyed (as I was informed, during the popular madness
of the reign of terror, 1793), and the prints remaining with Bervic torn in
pieces, in the savage intention of obliterating every vestige of royalty.
The fragments, however, had been fortunately preserved, and in quieter
times were put together again in so ingenious a manner that the previous
damage was not easily to be discovered.   I have one of the prints in this
restored state in my possession. His apartment in the Louvre was hung

stitute, the allowance to each being 1500 francs per annum, about
£60, and equivalent, the different expense of living considered, to
nearly £100 in England. David, whose name was in every body's
mouth as the great regenerator, or rather founder, of true taste
in art, I had not the good fortune to be introduced to. He
lived in a state of great seclusion, passing his time between
painting and music, performing well, as an amateur, as I understood, on the violoncello. His intimacy with Robespierre, and
his extreme revolutionary principles and extravagant conduct
as a member of the National Convention, in which he voted
for the death of the king, are well known, as also his narrow
escape, in consideration of his talents as an artist from that
death on the scaffold which many think he richly merited.[74]
At this time (1802) his " Rape of the Sabines " was exhibiting,
and was, I believe, the first instance of money being received
for admission to the view of a picture.   On that score a great
deal of clamour was raised against him by the Parisians, very
unjustly in my opinion, while the painting itself was lauded
by them to the skies, very unjustly also, as I think. It excited
a good deal of curiosity among the English visiters, which
ended in disappointment. The French people, thought to be
ever in extremes, certainly displayed the national volatility of

round with Woollet's finest landscapes, of which he spoke in raptures as
miracles d'harmonie. He possessed, I believe, some private fortune, and
was not necessitated to labour for mere existence ; and that he held his
art in very low estimation for such a purpose may be gathered from his
blunt observation to me one day. *" Mon jeune ami, c'est un vilain metier
que la gravure."*   He left unfinished at his death a large plate after a
picture in the Musée by Poussin ; *" Le Testament d'Eudamidas."*

[74] Exiled from France on the restoration of the Bourbons, he retired to
Brussels, where he died.

character in a striking degree, by their sudden and enthusiastic
adoption of that style of art introduced by David, and still
known as *L'Ecole Classique*. It is scarcely possible to conceive
a more decided contrast between it and its immediate pre-
cursor, the meretricious and flaunting mannerism of the school
of Boucher and his contemporaries. Another change has since
"come o'er the spirit of the age," and the Classic and the
Romantic are now struggling for the ascendency. Whether
the contest end in the absolute supremacy of the latter, or in
the combination of those qualities of each that may not be
heterogeneous, remains to be seen ; the result, however, will
probably be advantageous in either case to the interests of art.
No one will question the high degree of *power* possessed by
the French in every department of the fine arts : the doubt
seems to be principally as to the soundness of their judgment
in its application. To return to David's picture. It was
viewed by the English with a mixed feeling of surprise and
dissatisfaction at the novelty of its style, and at the audacity
with which its pretensions to excellence were put forward, in
opposition to the long and justly accredited authorities of the
old masters. The ostentatious and elaborated display of the
naked figure offended the habitual delicacy of those even who
were least fastidious. Republican simplicity, if it did not
introduce this meretricious system into the French school, certainly carried it to an excess hitherto unpractised in any other.[75]

75 This extravagance is now somewhat abated ; but several of the subjects in the truly national gallery of modern painters, founded some years
ago in the Luxembourg palace, exhibit abundant proof of the fact here
stated. The figure of Tatius in the Rape of the Sabines has, however,
undergone some alteration since its first exhibition. There are at present
in the same collection other large pictures by David, and also a good many

About this time, Gérard,[76] Gros,[77] Girodet,[78] Guérin,[79] and

by his celebrated pupils deceased, Guérin, Girodet, and Gros, some of which
have great and just claims to high commendation, and the whole together,
whatever may be its defects in detail, forms equally a subject for us to admire and imitate. Indeed it is quite impossible for an Englishman to quit
the gallery without a feeling of mortification and self-reproach that in England no advance has yet been made to promote so legitimate an object as
the establishment of a national collection of the works of British artists.

[76] Gérard. This gentleman, an Italian by birth, but a Frenchman by
adoption, habit, and long residence, is generally considered well entitled to
that station at the head of the art in France which had been occupied by
David. His pictures of the Entry of Henry IV. into Paris, Battle of Aus-
terlitz, Corinne, Psyche, Ossian, &c., are well known and deservedly admired. The first mentioned was greatly damaged, on account of its royalist
subject, by the infuriated populace in their irruption into the Louvre, in
July, 1830, (the three days of the second revolution). Gérard is of the
école classique; but with more of truth and nature, though, perhaps,
with less of power and originality than his immediate predecessor. Gérard
died in January (1837). His enfeebled sight had for some years interrupted his professional pursuits.

[77] Gros painted several large pictures of battles and events in Napoleon's
career, displaying considerable force of effect, with great bravura of execution. The painting of the *plafond* of St. Genevieve has many admirers
among the French, and obtained for the artist the title of Baron, specially
conferred on him by Charles X. while viewing the picture. Gros is supposed to have committed suicide; his body having been found in the Seine,
June 26th, 1835. He was in opulent circumstances, of eccentric character,
and, as I was told, (though I did not find him so) of harsh and repulsive
manners.

[78] Girodet's reputation stands high, and he had the honour of obtaining
the crown of victory in a competition with David and others. The Deluge
is one of the best known and most important of his performances. He died
in the prime of life.

[79] Guérin. Possessing more of elegance and refinement, with great
power of expression, his pictures in the Luxembourg gallery form an important and interesting part of the collection.

Prud'hon,[80] were making rapid progress to eminence, and a younger artist, Ingres,[81] was emerging from indigence and obscurity. But, whatever may be the worldly circumstances of an artist in France (and I believe that in pecuniary matters they are much alike in all places) it cannot escape observation, that in that country they are allowed to take a higher rank in public estimation, relatively to the other classes of society, than is permitted to them generally in England. The fact is undisputed, and indeed indisputable, and may perhaps be accounted for partly by the almost universal diffusion of a taste for the fine arts in France, and partly, I am inclined to think, to the absence of that aristocracy of wealth arising from our commercial supremacy, which bids fair in the long run to gain the absolute ascendency over, or to swamp, as the phrase is, those of birth, rank, virtue, or talent. It is interesting to observe the presence of the humbler classes and their decorous conduct in the numerous establishments open gratuitously to the public, and no one will deny the great and beneficial influence that must result from such facilities being so liberally and judiciously afforded. It is to be lamented that, in our own country, the national establishments and the national monuments are so hedged in with what are called vested rights, that they are, in effect, as a sealed book to the great mass of

[80] Prud'hon. This artist, with a purer taste in composition and better style of colouring than ordinarily belong to the French school, produced but little, and his works were not generally relished by his fellow-countrymen.

[81] Ingres — a member of the Institute, and successor to Horace Vernet as Director of the French Academy at Rome, 1836. He has not produced much, and his reputation, though high among artists and dilletanti, is limited to a small circle. He is an idolater and follower of the pure school of Raphael.

the community.   It is impossible to enter the Louvre, the
Bibliothèque, the Museum of Natural History, &c., &c., in
Paris, and not feel some degree of mortification at the striking
contrasts in this and many other respects, that are to be found
in similar institutions equally under the authority and control
of government, in France, and in England.[82]

Among the exhibitions of Paris open at this period was one
of great interest, though it could not be contemplated without
many painful reflections : namely, the collection of such monumental sculpture in the Petits-Augustins [83] as had escaped

[82] England has latterly made some advances to a more liberal mode of
conduct as regards these matters.

[83] This museum of antiquities no longer exists in an aggregate form, and
its dispersion caused some regrets.   The monuments have been mostly, and
without doubt very properly, restored to their former places in the various
cathedrals, abbeys, churches, and religious establishments, from whence
they had been sacrilegiously removed and defaced by the ungovernable
fury of the populace in 1793 and 1794.   St. Denis, the burial-place of a
line of kings; Notre Dame, St. Genevieve, and numerous other cemeteries,
had been thus desecrated, in the madness of the time ; the wonder now is
that the whole was not swept away by the resistless torrent of revolutionary
excitement.   As it is, great and irreparable injury has been sustained by
many of the finest works of art, though the mischief was greatly palliated
by the ingenuity that was promptly and skilfully brought into action.   Re-
placed, as I suppose they now are, according to their original destination,
they will be contemplated with those feelings of traditionary respect and
veneration that are invariably associated in the mind with consecrated antiquity.   Foreigners, who in such numbers visit the capital, and very many
of the Parisians themselves, would probably have preferred in this and
similar cases the concentration of individual and interesting objects in a
museum, but the principles of good feeling and sound policy were equally
in favour of the measure adopted.   Paris has long been considered poli-
tically too much as all France itself; and any just proceeding, limiting its
undue influence in the community, has, so far, an additional claim in its favour.

utter annihilation from the fury of the barbarian Iconoclasts of Republicanism run wild, in the year 1793. It had in part been rescued, and the whole brought together by the indefatigable exertions of M. Lenoir, an artist and antiquary of reputation, who had devoted his time and attention exclusively to this object, and to the historical and chronological arrangement of the monuments in separate halls of the old monastery, according to the eras of their respective execution. Many of them were sadly mutilated and defaced, while there was scarcely one that had not suffered some injury from the savage and wanton rage of the destroyers. Every statue, every sarcophagus that had a reference to monarchy or feudality, bore some marks of suffering from the worse than Vandal tide of destruction that had flowed over them. Not a word in any inscription relating to the royal dignity but had been coarsely though effectually obliterated from the sarcophagi, and the sacred ashes they enclosed scattered to the winds. I passed many hours of pleasing though sad reflection in the solemn stillness and dim religious light of some of the apartments of the old convent, and in " chewing the food of sweet and bitter fancy " as my eyes wandered o'er the imaged representatives of kings, heroes, and ministers, who have passed away " like the baseless fabric of a vision," after filling the earth with the pomp and glory of their living achievements.

The objects in this assemblage of sculptured records of times gone by were highly calculated to raise the sympathies of Englishmen, who with their pride of freedom combine, both in their feeling and practice, a disposition to honour exalted rank and distinguished genius.[84] Perhaps there is no country in Europe,

---

[84] This feeling was abundantly manifested by the numbers of our fellow-countrymen constantly to be seen at the Augustins.

despotic or otherwise, in which the aristocratical tendencies of
the people are so obviously displayed as in England. Each
class of society maintains a sort of line of demarcation between
itself and its subordinates, acting tacitly, but effectually, and
as thoroughly understood as it is quiescently submitted to and
rarely invaded. It may be witnessed in every degree; at most
times, and in all places; in public meeting, and in private
party; in church, and in playhouse; in stage-coach, and in
packet-boat; at a *table-d'hôte*, and at a corporation dinner; in
a seat at a coffee-house, and at a Vauxhall gala; and, even
where it might be thought impossible that it should be able to
show itself, even in a jury-box in the law-courts!

Though it will admit of a question whether it may not have been
advisable to replace the monuments in their originally destined
situation, a subject a good deal discussed, there can be no doubt
that, by the judicious measure of collecting them together, their
conservation at least was secured. Great credit was due to
the administrator of this museum, M. Alexandre Lenoir,[85] for
his courageous and persevering labour in preserving these venerable relics from the destroyers, wherein he encountered great
personal danger, and received a wound, the mark of which, as
he stated, would go with him to the grave. His classification
of the objects, according to their respective eras, was well
adapted to the purposes of study in history, chronology, and
the arts, beginning with the antique and Celtic remains, fol-

---

[85] Monsieur Lenoir was appointed to his office by a committee of the
National Assembly, when that representative body had decreed that the
possessions of the clergy appertained to the *chose publique*. He seems to
have been well qualified for the situation; of which, judging from his publications, he himself was thoroughly convinced. He took greatly to heart,
as I was informed afterwards, the breaking-up of the collection.

lowed by those of the middle age, and succeeded by those of the thirteenth and subsequent centuries. Of the antique there were some curious fragments, of some of which our cele-brated countryman, Flaxman,[86] made drawings in that pure and fine taste that so eminently distinguished him. These fragments were few in number, consisting of sacrificial altars, bas-reliefs, sepulchral stones, &c., and bearing in themselves strong evidence of their genuineness. Of the Celtic remains there were three or four rude sculptures, interesting only to antiquaries, and purporting to be of the time of the Gauls, under Tiberius.[87] Of the middle ages, from the seventh to the thirteenth centuries, the tombs of the earlier French monarchs, Dagobert, Clovis, Childebert, and more especially the sepulchral chapel of Abelard and Héloise,[88] made nearly the whole cata-logue of that period. The Hall [89] of the thirteenth century arrests

[86] John Flaxman is a name that will live long in Europe. His inspira-tion was drawn from Grecian art in its most palmy state. No man's works evince a greater knowledge or better application of the beauties of the antique than do those of Flaxman. His designs for Dante and Homer, his Shield of Achilles, and his various public monuments, are universally known and appreciated.

[87] Without presuming to question their authenticity, I may be allowed to remark that the monuments of the early ages, as they appeared in this museum, were in many instances rather a composition of scattered *débris* than the actual sepulchres, in the state they had previously existed, of the actual monarchs and other distinguished personages.

[88] The monument of Abelard and Héloise has now for many years formed an object of general interest at the cemetery of Père la Chaise. Like the others of the same period, it is a re-union of materials gathered from various sources.

[89] I am tempted to transcribe the subjoined extract, as highly character-istic of the respectable administrator, who on no occasion was disposed to put his light under a bushel. "Le premier consul Bonaparte, en visitant

the attention, both by the dawnings of art and its subjects, which are, however, by no means numerous, and consist chiefly of the monuments of that good and brave prince, Louis IX. and his family. Among them was that of his unworthy brother, Charles King of Sicily, who by his tyranny drove his subjects to revolt, and thereby caused the horrible massacre of the French on Easter day, 1277, known as the " Sicilian Vespers." In the next following division there is but little to excite remark. A marble statue, recumbent on a cenotaph, usually constituted the monumental arrangement of this period. Of this description is the tomb of King John the Good, who died in London in 1364, having been taken prisoner, with his son, by the Black Prince, at the battle of Poitiers, and that of Bertrand Duguesclin,[90] *le bon connétable*, a hero whose memory is cherished by the French with scarcely less affectionate remembrance than that of Henri Quartre. History records that he was not handsome in person, and his *effigies* in this monument

---

mon établissement, parut extrêmement satisfait de mes travaux, et il ne put s'empêcher de me le témoigner avec *son obligeance ordinaire;* il me dit, en entrant dans cette salle (13me siècle) qui lui représentait les édifices qu'il avoit parcouru dans son voyage d'Asie : ' *Lenoir, vous me transportez en Syrie ; je suis très content, continuez vos recherches, et j'en verrai toujours les résultats avec plaisir.'* "

[90] " From his earliest infancy, Duguesclin breathed but of combats. ' There is not a more mischievous boy in the world,' said his mother ; ' he is covered with bruises, his face scratched, always fighting, either beating others, or being beaten himself.' He was of low stature, strongly built ; with broad shoulders, and muscular arms ; with eyes small, but animated, and full of fire ; snubbed nose, and thick lips ; his whole physiognomy anything but agreeable. ' I am very ugly,' said he ; ' I shall never be a favourite of the ladies ; but I may perhaps be able to make myself feared by the enemies of my country.' "

go to verify the correctness of the historian. In the hall of the fifteenth century might be noticed the statue of Isabella of Bavaria, infamous for her crimes: of Jeanne d'Arc : of Charles VI. : Charles VII. : &c. but of little interest as works of art. The reign of Francis I. forms an epoch in the progress of civilization and refinement. His chivalric character, bordering on romance, and his taste for magnificence, harmonized with that spirit of the time which had been brought into activity in *le siècle de la renaissance*. By his invitation, Leonardo da Vinci and Primaticcio were attached to his court ; and the protection afforded by his government to the fine arts was well illustrated by their great and rapid advance towards perfection. The works of Pierre Lescot, Bullant, Philibert de Lorme, in architecture; Jean Goujon,[91] Germain Pilon, and Jean Cousin, in sculpture, are ample confirmation of the splendid productions of the sixteenth century. The degradation of pure classic taste in the seventeenth century is marked by the then popular works in painting, sculpture, and architecture of Simon Vouet, Bernini, Borromini, &c. who, with great qualifications in their respective pursuits, allowed themselves to be seduced from the transcendent standard of excellence, in the delusive hope of superadding still greater charms of grace and spirit. One of the prevailing fancies of the time was that of making copies with *improvements* of the antique statues ! Many of these misdirected efforts are still to be seen in the gardens at the Tuileries and at Versailles. The hall of the seventeenth century abounds

[91] Jean Goujon, called the French Phidias, one of the victims in the massacre of St. Bartholomew's Day, was killed by a shot from an arquebuse while working on his scaffold at the Louvre. His exquisite bas-reliefs in the "Fontaine des Innocents," and some colossal figures and bas-reliefs in the old Louvre, are universally known and admired.

with the splendid labours of Girardon, Coysevox, Puget, and
Sarrazin, and contained, among many others well deserving attention, the magnificent monuments of Cardinals Richelieu [92]
and Mazarin, those of Colbert, Turenne, De Thou, and Lebrun,
the painter. Of the sculpture of the eighteenth century, I noticed several fine works by Pigalle, Bouchardon, and Coustou,
but no monument of importance, except that of Marshal
Count Harcourt. This last division was, on the whole, the
least interesting of the collection.

The general effect of this magnificent assemblage of sculpture
was much heightened by many fine specimens of stained glass,
so judiciously placed as greatly to assist the impression which
the monuments were themselves calculated to produce. It is
to be lamented that painting on glass seems in a fair way of
adding to the number of the lost arts. In concluding this
lengthened notice of the Musée des Monumens, I would observe that it formed (after the accumulated glories of the
Louvre) the most captivating scene for contemplation that
could be witnessed in Paris.

In the list of public institutions, that of the Bibliothèque
is justly held in high estimation by foreigners and as an object
of well-founded national pride by Frenchmen. It has the reputation of being the most complete in Europe, superior even
to that of the Vatican; while the national urbanity is amply
shewn, in the facilities of study and reference, to students and
foreigners. Among its other treasures is a collection of medals ;
those of gold of the Lower Empire (I believe) are of surpassing

[92] It was in his endeavours to rescue this monument from the attacks of
some revolutionary soldiers that M. Lenoir received a bayonet-wound in
his hand, the mark of which, to use his own words as before stated, he
should carry to the grave.

beauty. To this may be added an unequalled cabinet of engravings, ancient and modern ; the collossal globes of Coronelli ;
the curious model of the French Parnassus, &c. The effect
produced by the great extent of the establishment, the admirable order of its arrangements, the number of readers, and the
remarkable stillness of the whole scene, were very striking.

The Jardin des Plantes, including the Ménagerie and the
Cabinet of Natural History, was a never-failing object of attraction both to strangers and residents. At this period, the
Ménagerie contained the usual assortment of animals, and an
elephant of enormous bulk, one of a pair that had been in the
Stadtholder's collection at the Hague, and transferred by right
of conquest to Paris. The male had recently died, and I believe
his companion did not long survive. Their keeper, an Englishman, had been made prize of along with them ; and, in
relating these incidents, and commenting on the despotic power
of Bonaparte, which had forced not only the Stadtholder's ele-
phants to come to Paris, but their keeper to accompany them,
contrived to turn the sympathies of his fellow-countrymen to
some account. This establishment has been since greatly extended and improved in all its departments, particularly in that
of the Cabinet of Natural History.

Although the horrors and tumults of an infuriated anarchy
had entirely passed away, and the stillness and order of a military government [93] had now succeeded, there were still remaining some vestiges of the revolutionary torrent that had swept
over the land. On the principal front of the palace of the

[93] With regard to the individuals of the military class that came under
my notice, I found their manners decidedly more civilized and more urbane
than those of the community in general. The consciousness of power and
their triumphant career might have produced this effect.

Tuileries was inscribed, in many places where the cannon-balls had struck, " 10 Août," in commemoration of the triumphant attack of the armed populace on the 10th of August, 1792, which ended in the overthrow of the monarchy. During what the French call the *temps de la terreur*, many of the churches were desecrated by various occupations of trade and manufacture. Most of these had been restored to their sacred destination by the " wisdom and benign authority" (as I have heard it described by a Frenchman) of the first consul, though some few continued to be used as warehouses and stables. Adjoining my hotel, in the Rue Mont Orgueil, was one occupied by a saddler, in which the usual stock-in-trade of harness, collars, whips, &c., were displayed on the walls. The sabbath was, however, as far as I observed, but little devoted to the exercise of public worship, the churches being but thinly attended, and chiefly by aged women ; and the neglected and dirty state of many of the most venerable edifices, and in which decency and propriety were little observed, formed a striking contrast to an eye accustomed to the neatness, good order, and religious feeling that are witnessed in our happy country.[94]   Many shops were kept

---

[94] I had an opportunity of seeing a grand display of the Roman Catholic ceremonial in the church of Notre Dame, on the occasion of an uncle of the first consul's (Cardinal Fesch) being consecrated Archbishop of Paris. The whole scene was very splendid, very imposing, and seemed to be considered very theatrical by all parties, more especially by the principal performer, the cardinal. The ladies of Bonaparte's family were present at the ceremony, and constituted the most interesting part of the shew. The first consul did not appear ; indeed, he was seldom seen in public at this time. I was much struck with the handsome, dignified, and expressive countenance of the mother (Madame Mère, as she was called). She was then, I believe, about fifty. The church was crowded, and foreigners mustered in great numbers, particularly the English. Military officers (in

open on Sundays, and business carried on as usual ; but amusement was, after all, the principal business, and the general
character and aspect of the day were more gay and holiday-like
than ordinary, the theatres and places of public entertainment
being crowded with the working classes. Another indication
of that change that had " frighted the land from her propriety "
was the occasional use of the word " citoyen," I having myself
had the honour to be so addressed by a man who had the appearance of a decent mechanic : the military class had, however,
resumed the aristocratic term of " monsieur." Small tricoloured cockades were generally worn in the hat, partly covered
by the band. Englishmen were still sometimes accosted, when
an object of interest was in view, with the flattering and nearly
obsolete title of " milor."

Paris abounds with objects that engage the attention and
excite the interest of strangers in an extraordinary degree ; but
the sight which stimulated public curiosity at this time beyond
every thing else was that of the " observed of all observers,"
the first consul himself ! As my stay in Paris was at first
meant to be about ten days or a fortnight at the utmost (though
it extended, in fact, to two months), I had but small hopes of
success in this matter, more especially as Bonaparte seldom
appeared but at a review or at a theatre, and at the latter always
without any previous announcement. I made some attempts
at the Opera and Théâtre Français, at times when, according
to the rumour of the day, the presence of the first consul was
expected ; but they ended in disappointment. However, I did

uniform) had seats appropriated to them ; and two or three of our countrymen of the guards in their scarlet and gold contributed to the brilliance of
the *coup d'œil*.

ultimately succeed in obtaining a view of this modern Attila, as
he has been designated. He was accustomed, at intervals, to
review the troops forming the garrison of Paris in the open space
(Place du Carousel) in front of the Tuileries ; and here I
secured a place for six francs at a first-floor window of a house
under repair, that abutted on one end of the ground, and afforded
a commanding sight of the whole. The soldiers were ranged
in lines the entire length of the place, and, consisting as they
did of the *élite* of the infantry, and amounting, as I was told,
to six or seven thousand men, all in their best appointments,
they certainly made, under the glow of a bright day in August,
a spectacle that the French might well feel proud of. The
company of sappers, with their picturesque beards, snow-white
leather aprons, and polished steel axes glancing in the meridian
sun, attracted especial notice.

Precisely at twelve o'clock, the first consul descended the
great staircase of the *château*, and, mounting his favourite white
horse, and surrounded by a numerous *état-major*, among whom
the Mameluke Roustan was conspicuous by his eastern costume, was saluted with military honours, music, drums, trum-
pets, and the shouts of the assembled multitude. After some
preliminary inspection, which occupied nearly an hour, Bonaparte rode up and down the respective lines at a hand-canter,
accompanied by his brilliant staff, all glittering in golden splendour. He himself was dressed in a blue uniform, entirely destitute of ornament, plain cocked hat, white pantaloons, and
jockey-boots—boots with tops—and was a little in advance of
his company. As he approached the end of the line that was
within a few yards of my station, I had a very distinct view of
his person ; and it made that kind of impression on me that the
recollection of it is still fresh in my memory at the moment I

am now writing—a lapse of five and thirty years. He appeared small in person, *thin*, of a placid, grave expression, and a complexion of a clear, yellowish brown, quite equal and unvaried in colour. When the inspection was finished, he rode to the centre, and shortly addressing the soldiers saluted them, and passed under the archway of the palace; the troops filed off, and the review terminated.

It was impossible to avoid remarking the deep and universal feeling of pride and admiration with which the French regarded their youthful hero — he was then about thirty-two years old, but looked scarcely so much, perhaps from the slightness of his figure. Of about twenty-five persons collected on benches raised one above another in the window and balcony where I sat, there was no foreigner but myself; and, from the price of admission, the individuals might be fairly considered generally of a respectable station. Of this company, there was not one that did not loudly and enthusiastically express his sentiments in favour of the restorer and promoter of the *glory* of their country. This, perhaps, is not an unfair instance of the predominating spirit of the nation, and naturally leads to the reflection of how powerful and how formidable such a spirit must render such a people! After the review — parade was the French term for it—Bonaparte held a *levée*, or *réception*, which was numerously attended, chiefly by military and foreigners, Englishmen mustering in great numbers.

Whether it be from living in a more genial climate, or from inherent disposition, or from other various and concurrent causes, it is certain that the French are a less domestic people than their nearest neighbours. "*An Englishman's fireside*" has no equivalent in France either in word or deed. Hence the innumerable coffee-houses and *restaurateurs*; the crowded promenades, and public gardens; the Boulevards, the Tuileries, the Palais Royal, the Luxembourg, the numerous theatres and places of entertainment which distinguish Paris above all other capitals in Europe, and almost warrant the belief that pleasure is the only business steadily pursued by Frenchmen. The national observation is well known, " that there is but one Palais Royal in the world ;" and Paris may, perhaps, justly claim to be the capital city and head-quarters of amusement. Paris has been said to comprehend all France, and the Palais Royal all Paris. Certainly, no one could fail of being impressed with the scene that this far-famed Orléans palace presents, on a summer's evening in particular. The beauty of the gardens, the elegance of the building, the splendour of the *cafés* and various shops, the gaming and reading-rooms on the first story, all blazing with light, the convenience of its situation in the best part of Paris, and the " busy hum" of the gay crowds there drawn together, have been often described, though, in description, giving but a very inadequate idea of the reality.

It was here that, in the troubled times of the Revolution, the demoniac spirit of that tremendous political convulsion first poured forth its incendiary and bloodthirsty doctrines to its ready and well-prepared instruments. The infuriated Camille Desmoulins, mounted on a chair, and, with a pistol in each hand, addressing an excited multitude day after day ; the deliberate assassination of the deputy of the Convention, Le Pelletier, while at dinner at Fevrier's, the *restaurateur ;* the refined cruelty of the populace in making the wretched Egalité (Duc d'Orléans [95]) stop some minutes before his own palace

[95] Louis Philippe Joseph, Duke of Orléans, father of the present King of the French, passed some time in England (when Duc de Chartres) about

when drawn in a cart to execution: these are a few of the events, among many, that give to the Palais Royal its worst celebrity. Among the changes made by the Revolution was that of the names of places; as Palais du Tribunat for Palais Royal: this was the title it bore in 1802, arising from the circumstance of one of the new legislative bodies (the Tribunat) holding their sittings in the palace. By means of an acquaintance, I had an opportunity of being present at a meeting of this branch of the constitution, but it had little to interest a stranger, either in the individuals of which it was then composed, or by the acts which emanated from it. It was a mere instrument in the master-hand of Bonaparte, and was soon altogether absorbed in his overwhelming power. A man of some notoriety (Lewis Goldsmith [96]), with whom I had become slightly acquainted in

the year 1786, and became intimate with the Prince of Wales (George IV.). Sir Joshua Reynolds painted a whole-length portrait of him for the prince, which was unfortunately destroyed, with several other of Sir Joshua's finest works, by an accidental fire at Carlton House. When d'Orléans voted in the Convention for the death of Louis XVI., this portrait was removed from its station by order of the Prince of Wales, and was never afterwards seen in public, except during an exhibition of Sir Joshua's works at the British Gallery in Pall-Mall. The duke was represented in a scarlet hussar uniform, and the picture was considered as one of the very finest of this great artist's works. Indeed, after its destruction, it was by some of the best judges discovered to be the most magnificent, the most perfect portrait that the art had ever produced.

[96] Lewis Goldsmith was born and bred a Jew, but quitted that religion without adopting any other. He had been in some mercantile concern, and was bankrupt. He published in England a book full of sedition, with the title *The Crimes of Cabinets.* In Paris he established an English newspaper called *The Argus,* for the chief, if not the only, purpose of maligning and vilifying England and its government, and was connected with all the Irish and English of desperate character and fortune that had been vomited

London, introduced me, and pointed out some of the men of
the Revolution ; but as they were but second or third-rate
personages, but little interest or curiosity was excited. Goldsmith seemed to be on familiar terms with several of them.

The *salons littéraires* (reading-rooms) were among the most
respectable and most agreeable of the Palais Royal lounges.
For a very moderate remuneration, the subscribers were supplied with the newspapers, foreign and native, together with
the principal political pamphlets of the day. The opportunity
afforded in these establishments of conversing with intelligent
and well-educated Frenchmen (always a desirable and useful
object) was an advantage not to be overlooked, more especially
as their feelings at that time were not exasperated against England by that mortified pride and disappointed ambition which
subsequent events engendered. Among our countrymen that
I met with occasionally at this place, the names of Holcroft,[97]

from their native land. It was supposed that he had made himself serviceable in some way or other to the ruling powers in France; but he did not
continue long in favour; he either did not satisfy his employers, or was
disappointed in his expectations from them. He contrived, however, to
obtain permission to return to England, and immediately set to work to pull
his old master (Napoleon) to pieces, with at least as much apparent relish
as he had formerly shown in upholding him. He was in London in 1823-4,
but I finally lost view of him soon afterwards.

[97] Thomas Holcroft. This extraordinary man, author of *The Road to
Ruin* and other successful plays, originally a Newmarket jockey, then an
actor, then political writer, associated with Horne Tooke, Hardy, Thelwall,
and, tried with them for high treason, was at this time in Paris, where he
remained a year or two preparing those travels which were afterwards
published in two quarto volumes by Sir Richard Phillips. He had two
grown-up daughters, and had recently married a second wife, a young
Frenchwoman, by whom he had several children. He was of a most petulant and irritable temper, which I had frequent opportunities of observing

Underwood,[98] and Duppa,[99] are not unknown. The two latter, imprudently lengthening their stay in France, were caught, as in a net, by Bonaparte's decree of detention as prisoners of war at Verdun of all the English then in France. I was fortunate in having quitted Paris before matters had proceeded to extremities ; but symptoms of great irritation and bad understanding between the governments had already shewn themselves in abundance, giving ample warning to the prudent and the sensitive to retreat in time.

The English journals had scarcely relaxed at all since the peace in their abuse of the first consul ; and a most severe and ably-written attack upon him appearing in the *Morning Chronicle* (August, 1802) so inflamed his wrath, that an order was instantly issued, prohibiting the admission into France of the whole mass of our newspapers. This, of course, would be felt

while playing for amusement with him at billiards, forming a most striking contrast with my preconceived notions of his philosophy founded on his writings. He was a good deal acquainted among artists, and intimate with Opie.

[98] Thomas Richard Underwood, draughtsman to the Antiquarian Society, and a clever painter in water-colours. He had a good deal of scientific acquirement, was a tolerable chemist and geologist, and, having an independence, pursued nothing as a profession. He married when very young a Miss Stageldoir, a dancer at Drury Lane Theatre, from whom he soon separated. He died at Auteuil, near Paris, in 1836, and was stated to have offered, in his last illness, to submit to a most severe surgical operation, if there had been a reasonable probability of his life being lengthened a few weeks, that he might have had an opportunity of witnessing the return of Halley's comet.

[99] William Duppa, a lawyer of well-informed mind, and pleasant, gentlemanly manners, brother to Richard Duppa, the historian of Michael Angelo. I have always regretted never having afterwards met with William Duppa. He probably died abroad.

as a great privation, by Englishmen in particular, and indicated
pretty clearly the unfriendly spirit which prevailed at this time
in the French councils. Other circumstances also were not
wanting to confirm this view of the state of matters between
the two countries ; and, at the British embassy, in answer to
inquiries bearing upon the subject, a return home as soon as
convenient was advised. These signs and tokens were, notwithstanding, disregarded by great numbers, who in consequence
had many severe and vexatious hardships to encounter. Mr.
Hayes,[100] the retired bookseller, who had, from preference to
the country, removed his whole family, consisting of six persons, from England, was on the list of *détenus* ; but, from having fixed his residence in France, was allowed to remain with
his children in Paris, under the surveillance of the police, and
subject to occasional domiciliary visits from the authorities,
attended altogether with great expense to him, besides the
inconvenience and mortification. The enforcement of the decree
was gradually relaxed, and many of the prisoners found their
way back to England. Mr. Hayes and family returned to
London in 1809. Underwood became habituated to the

[100] Samuel Hayes, a classical bookseller, whose small fortune was much
reduced, I believe, by his compelled residence in Paris, after the renewal
of the war following the short peace of Amiens. The difficulty of obtaining
remittances at all from England, and, when obtained, the cruel diminution
they had undergone in unavoidable expenses, rendered that which was at
first calculated upon as a cheap country to live in quite the reverse. When
Mr. Hayes returned to England, he resumed, in partnership with his youngest
son, the business of a bookseller, in the knowledge of which, in his peculiar
department, he was said to be nearly unrivalled. His eldest son, Mr.
John Hayes, was brought up as an artist in the *atelier* of Monsieur Vincent
and others of the French school, and now practises with success as a portrait-painter in London.

French mode of living, and made only an occasional short visit to England. I heard of Duppa's having obtained permission to go, under surveillance, to Switzerland, but afterwards I lost sight of him altogether.

For a people who live so little at home as the French, the numerous *restaurateurs* and *cafés* of all degrees in the Palais Royal, by their accommodations, contribute greatly, in addition to the other various attractions of the place, to keep in full flow that tide of animated existence which Dr. Johnson remarked of Fleet Street. These establishments have been too often described to need any particular notice; but I cannot refrain from mentioning the delicious ices and *liqueurs rafraichissantes* which, during the great heats of July and August, refreshed the thirsty palate at a very moderate charge. There is a much greater consumption of them in France than in England, while, in regard to strong and spirituous drinks, the reverse will be found to exist. Indeed, I happened to see but one intoxicated person during the two months I passed in Paris; though I believe they have since somewhat degenerated from that habit of temperance which is so deserving of our imitation. I dined once at Very's, the well-known *restaurateur*, in the Palais Royal with a party of English, which I should not have noticed but that one part of the entertainment was a dish of frogs. It was the first and last time that I ever met with this famous *fricassée*, though I had previously seen the hind-quarters of the animals, (the only part eaten) prepared for the kitchen, floating in tubs in the markets. I did not much like the flavour, though I was not aware of what I was eating at the time, hearing it called a dish of *petits poulets*. It was rather a high-priced regale, and tasted more like rabbit than any thing else to which I could compare it—exceedingly insipid.

The Theatre Montansier, as it was then called, in the Palais Royal had but an indifferent reputation, arising rather from the discreditable character of its numerous female frequenters, than from any thing improper or deficient in its representations. Two of the actors, Brunet[101] and Tiercelin, possessed much comic humour and ability, and the former retained his popularity to an advanced age. Tiercelin left the stage, having acquired a moderate competency at a comparatively early period. The gaming-rooms form a striking feature in the number of *authorised* temptations at the Palais Royal. The destructive vice of gaming seems more generally diffused in Paris than in London; it certainly is more openly practised. While the government derives a considerable revenue from this as well as from other abominations, it will not readily be suppressed, however it may be condemned by the moralist. All classes may in Paris ruin themselves and families at games of hazard without the smallest restraint; but the most revolting circumstance attending these orgies is the presence of females. Young and handsome women, and indeed women of all ages,[102] may be seen, with countenances haggard and distorted under the agonizing influence of the hazards of the game, risking their last three francs or five francs on the chances of *la roulette.*

[101] Brunet was playing, with much of the public approbation, within these few years at the Théâtre des Varietés, on the Boulevards at Paris. Tiercelin had a great deal of broad, farcical humour, the effect of which was irresistibly laughable. His only daughter is married to Perlet, the celebrated comedian.

[102] There are many women in Paris whose chief occupation is gaming, and who are known as and are called *joueuses.* On the Paris Stock Exchange, also, numbers of women may be seen whose constant employment is speculating in a small way in the public funds.

Such a scene as this surely could not be witnessed in England, though gaming on a great scale is perhaps as prevalent or even more so in London than it is in Paris. So much for the Palais Royal.

Among the *agrémens* of Paris, the dinner at a *table d'hôte* should not be forgotten ; and, notwithstanding the accommodation and convenience of the *restaurants*, I found the *table d'hôte* still more agreeable, inasmuch as it was a sort of introduction into French society. Though in principle not unlike an English " ordinary," it was in practice a much more refined and elegant repast. While in England nearly the whole attention of the landlord or landlady is occupied in cutting up the substantial joints of meat for their customers, that of the French *hôte* or *hôtesse* (but little carving being required) is not merely engaged in watchful anticipation of the wishes of their guests, and active superintendence of the servants, but, by a ready and judicious exercise of those powers of conversation which distinguish the French above all other nations, prevent those awful and distressing pauses that seem like suspended animation, and which are constantly recurring in the solemnities of an English dinner. In short, the *hôte* assumes for the time being the character of a gentleman at his own table, surrounded by his friends, to whom it is his duty, more from a point of honour than of interest, to render the entertainment worthy of himself and satisfactory to his guests. From being rather more expensive, and each individual having generally some sort of introduction, the company is, of course, more select than it could well be at a *restaurateur's*. *Tables d'hôtes* were not numerous at the time of my first visit to Paris, and they have since become still more rare. Where I most frequently dined was at the Hotel Ventadour, Rue Ventadour ; and there it was that

I made, among others, the acquaintance of Gaetano Bartolozzi,[103] and met with Clementi,[104] the celebrated composer, and his pupil Field, when starting on their extensive continental tour. Few men ever had greater influence in their time for good or evil than Thomas Paine. As the able and active disseminator of those democratic and irreligious principles which, though apparently crushed and extinguished,

> " Still in their ashes burn their wonted fires,"

and threaten from time to time to set the world again in a revolutionary blaze, this extraordinary man was a subject of interest

[103] Gaetano Stephen Bartolozzi, son of the eminent engraver, inherited none of his father's distinguished talent as an artist, but resembled him perhaps too much in that indolent facility of disposition which made them both easy victims to the artful and interested designs of others. The younger Bartolozzi was an enthusiast in music, and a good amateur performer on the violin (tenor). This passion led to his marriage with Miss Jansen, the daughter of a dancing-master of Aix-la-Chapelle. The lady was a pupil of Clementi, and considered to be one of the best of his school. The marriage was not a happy one, and Gaetano, after many vicissitudes, died in great poverty. He left two daughters : the elder, Lucy, Madame Vestris, the popular actress; the younger, Josephine, married to a Mr. Anderson, a singer.

[104] Clementi is, I believe, considered by musicians as a genius of a high order, and the founder of the modern system of pianoforte music. I heard Pleyel, the German composer, who at that time kept a music-shop in Paris, mention Clementi as a truly great master in his peculiar province. Clementi was well-informed, intelligent, and spoke English almost like a native. John Field, his celebrated pupil, was, when quite a boy, thought to be the finest player in the world. He settled at St. Petersburgh, where he died in 1836. He made a short visit to England a few years before his death, and gave a concert which produced no results. Probably his style of playing is less appreciated since the introduction of Moscheles, Hertz, &c.

and curiosity both in what he had been and in what he had become. He was now a fallen meteor — poor, friendless, and almost dependent for his daily bread upon the casual bounty of some of his compassionate fellow-countrymen. He was at this time constantly to be seen at an obscure *cabaret* in an obscure street in the fauxbourg St. Germain (Café Jacob, Rue Jacob). The scene, as we entered the room from the street—it was on the ground-floor—was, under the circumstances, somewhat impressive. It was on a summer's evening, and several of the tables were occupied by men, apparently tradesmen and mechanics, some playing at the then universal game of dominoes, others drinking their bottle of light, frothy, but pleasant beer, or their little glass of liqueur, while in a retired part of the room sat the once-dreaded demagogue, the supposed conspirator against thrones and altars, the renowned Thomas Paine! He was in conversation with several well-dressed Irishmen, who soon afterwards took leave, and we placed ourselves at his table. His general appearance was mean and poverty-stricken. The portrait of him engraved by Sharp from Romney's picture is a good likeness; but he was now much withered and care-worn, though his dark eye still retained its sparkling vigour. He was fluent in speech, of mild and gentle demeanour, clear and distinct in enunciation, and his voice exceedingly soft and agreeable. The subject of his talk of course being political, resembled very much his printed opinions; and the dogmatic form in which he delivered them seemed to evince his own perfect self-conviction of their truth. Among many predictions that subsequent events have not verified, he expressed himself quite confident that the Bank of England would never resume cash payments. Paine had been a member of the National Convention; and it is pleasant to know, as an Englishman, that on the trial of Louis XVI., he voted for the king's being pardoned. He was imprisoned during the time of terror, and narrowly escaped with his life. He had now sunk into complete insignificance, and was quite unnoticed by the government. I understood afterwards that Colonel Bosville, of Yorkshire, had shewn him great kindness, and enabled him to return to America, where he dragged out the few remaining years of his life in neglect and poverty.

In every capital city the theatres and places of public amusement constitute perhaps, in addition to their inherent entertainment, the readiest means whereby the passing and casual visiter may acquire some notion of the general manners and habits of a people. Judging from the number of playhouses, thronged for the most part by crowds of delighted spectators, the French may be fairly set down as the greatest playgoers in Europe. There were, in 1802, upwards of twenty theatres of various kinds open in Paris every night, Sunday not excepted, being a larger number than London, Vienna, Berlin, St. Petersburgh, Madrid, Naples, and Amsterdam possessed together, while the population of these seven capitals was in the aggregate full four times as numerous as that of the French metropolis.[105] If the opinion of Rousseau be well-founded, " that dramatic representations corrupt the morals, smooth the path to vice, and create a taste for frivolous pursuits," the nation can scarcely escape being very immoral, very vicious, and very trifling.

At the head of the list of theatres in Paris, viewed both as a splendid spectacle and as a national establishment, must be

[105] As regards London, this disproportion has long ceased to exist. Whether the moral character of our present population confirms or weakens the dogma of Jean Jacques I do not pretend to determine.

placed the Grand Opéra, or, as it was then called, (1802) Théâtre de la République et des Arts. It has peculiar claims to be considered as a national establishment, inasmuch as a large sum is annually supplied by the government to enable the managers to maintain its pre-eminence as the first theatre in Europe; a distinction certainly well merited in regard to its gorgeous and expensive decorations, and its numerous company of their best singers and unequalled dancers. Their principal singer, Laïs, had great power and compass of voice, which he had cultivated with assiduity and perseverance, and a firm, imposing style of execution that enchanted his countrymen at least, who held him to be quite without a rival. He was almost the only one worth naming, the female part of the company being at this time more than usually deficient. Madame Maillard, after the recent retirement of Mademoiselle St. Huberti,[106] was put forward in the first line, but proved utterly incompetent to the situation. Laïs appeared to great advantage in the part of Anacreon in the magnificent opera of that name; and its beautiful scenery and music rendered it a very favourable specimen of the performances of this theatre. Of the *ballet*, as a spectacle of action and dancing, it was beyond all comparison superior to any thing of the kind that I had ever seen. Eight or ten first-rate dancers, including Vestris, Deshayes, Beaulieu, with Madame Gardel, Clotilde, Boyeldieu, and a numerous and efficient *corps de ballet*, produced a result that set all competition at defiance. An English hornpipe

[106] This lady quitted the stage altogether on her marriage with the Sicilian count. Her melancholy fate will be remembered in England. She and her husband were murdered in their villa at Barnes Common, where they were residing, by an Italian domestic, who afterwards committed suicide. This happened about the year 1806.

G

danced by Beaupré in the dress of a jockey excelled every thing
of the kind that I had ever seen in England.

The Théâtre Français — De la République as it was still
called in 1802 — was the classic theatre, in which were represented the pure tragedy and comedy of Molière, Corneille,
Racine, and Voltaire, acted by the successors of Lekain,
Baron, Préville, and Mademoiselle Clairon, of the last age. Of
the old school, as it might be then called, I saw Monvel,[107] who
had enjoyed an enviable celebrity in his day, but was become
inferior from years and decay. Notwithstanding the loss of
teeth, his declamation was still much admired by the French,
but appeared to an English ear too elaborate and monotonous.
In person he was tall and thin, with rather harsh features ; his
enunciation was clear and distinct, his voice soft and agreeable,
and his action free and graceful, though somewhat redundant.
Another eminent actor, Dugazon[108], with whose performance
in comedy I was delighted, might also be considered as belonging to the old school. He was a great favourite with the
Parisians, and allowed to be a *parfait comique*, though a little
given to exaggeration in his acting, which, however well founded
the charge might have been in Frenchmen, was not perceptible
to me. Mademoiselle Mars was then beginning that successful

[107] Monvel had been educated, I believe, for the bar, and was an author
of no mean pretensions, as his play of *L'Amant bourru* and others of merit
sufficiently testify. During the French revolution he was noted for his
irreligion, and once addressed a numerous auditory from the pulpit of
St.-Roch, in a kind of sermon replete with blasphemy and impiety.

[108] Dugazon had also the bad reputation of having acted a rather pro-
minent part in the Revolution as a member of the Jacobin Club ; but these
recollections produced no ill effect upon the fortunes or popularity of the
actors.

career which has continued without interruption for nearly forty years, and with a popularity progressively increasing. Her earliest efforts, though always elegant and correct, were not considered by the French critics as indicating those commanding talents and that exquisite refinement in her art that, by the universal voice, have established her as without a rival in Europe.[109] I saw her but once at that time, and in the character of La fausse Agnès, in Destouches' comedy, from which Arthur Murphy has borrowed the plot in his farce of *The Citizen.* Her performance was replete with grace and good taste. Talma, the great tragedian, was then in the vigour of his age and full maturity of his powers : educated, if not born in England, (son of a respectable French dentist, who resided in Duke Street, Manchester Square) he had availed himself, while following out his vocation to the histrionic art, of frequent opportunities of witnessing the performances of our matchless Siddons, in Lady Macbeth, Isabella, Belvidera, &c., and, with the true tact of genius, had studied with incalculable advantage the principles of those extraordinary effects produced by the efforts of our greatest of performers. The result was something like a revolution in the system of acting in France. Co-operating with the fine tragedies of Voltaire, who had introduced, from his study of Shakspere, an energy and action hitherto unknown in the French drama, Talma almost entirely got rid of that stately, monotonous declamation, which rendered French heroics the most insipid of entertainments to foreigners. Talma had wrought other reforms in the French theatre, more espe-

[109] Mademoiselle Mars's talents are well known in England by her admirable performances in the French drama at Covent Garden Theatre and at the Opera House. She is still (1837) the delight of the theatrical amateurs of Paris.

cially in matters of costume; for the correctness of which, both in regard to its chronology and its exactitude, he had assiduously searched the best authorities. Mr. Kemble, whom I had met once or twice in Paris, and who, before his departure, was complimented by a splendid dinner given in his honour by the members of the French stage, had become a great admirer of Talma's acting, and was thought to have profited in some respects by his intimacy with him. Certainly, in one part, common to both these eminent men, I witnessed, after Mr. Kemble's return to England, a decided change in the manner in which he dressed the character, Orestes namely, in *The Distressed Mother*, by his adoption of the costume of Talma.[110]

The Opéra Comique was in 1802 a favourite and popular resort of the French, and with reason, for a better appointed company of performers, or a more enlivening choice of performances, did not exist, though it has since much degenerated. The names of Elleviou and Martin, the paragons of their class, are still quoted as standards of excellence, by which all talent of the same kind is to be measured and all eminent success to be compared. Elleviou [111] with a highly prepossessing and

---

[110] Talma always shewed much attachment to the English nation; and his hospitable table was very freely opened to our countrymen visiting Paris, though his known liberality on this head exposed him to some by no means flattering rencontres with certain individuals, who had no other claim to his notice than that of numbering themselves members of the same profession. He died in 1826, in circumstances far from affluent.

[111] Elleviou was a man of polished manners, and well received in good society. He was much esteemed in private life, and with some difficulty obtained, rather early, his permission to retire from the stage when his reputation was at its zenith.

very handsome person combined a fine voice, knowledge of music, and, above all, a degree of excellence as an actor that of itself alone would have placed him in the first rank of his profession. Martin,[112] to a voice of great compass and richness of tone, united an exquisite taste and profound science. In appearance he was not remarkable, and his acting was indifferent; but he had his partisans, who asserted his claims to superiority over all competitors; and he was certainly in great and general favour with the public, which he retained to the last.

Of the minor theatres, that of the Vaudeville had been very popular, and presented an exceedingly agreeable entertainment, and of a description essentially and peculiarly French. No species of dramatic representation in France seemed to me so entirely captivating as the Vaudeville. It is *sui generis*, and the attempts made to naturalize it on the English stage have almost invariably failed. The principal actor at the Vaudeville in 1802 was Laporte,[113] who had obtained a reputation by his performance, chiefly of the French harlequin—a very different kind of personage from the nimble gentleman of our Christmas pantomime—whom he resembles only in dress. The English hero is quite silent, and runs about with great activity; the French harlequin, on the contrary, moves but slowly, and talks a good deal, and generally outwits his seniors and superiors by a combination of affected simplicity and real cunning. The

112 In 1825, Martin appeared occasionally on the boards of the Opéra Comique. His powers were quite in their decline; but the public were most cordial in their reception of him, doubtless from their remembrance of what he had been.

113 Laporte has since played with some effect in England at the theatre in Tottenham Street, when occupied by a French company under the management of his son, the enterprising lessee of the Opera House.

famous Italian, Carlin,[114] of Bergamo, had previously acquired
a celebrity in this kind of character, which has proved quite
unattainable by his successors. This theatre had always been
a favourite of the French public, though not so much followed
at this period as it had been. The manager, M. Barré, was
himself the chief support of the concern, being the author of
many of the very best pieces that were brought forward : such
as *Les deux Edmons*,[115] *La Maison en Loterie*, &c. However in-
applicable the system of division of labour may be thought to
the production of works of mental excellence, it may be noticed
that many of the most successful specimens in this small literature are the offspring of two, three, and even as many as four
co-operators on one and the same subject. The ordinary *col-
laborateurs* of Barré were Radet, Desfontaines, and Piis, with
one or more of whom his name is constantly associated in the
title-page of his works.

A second Théâtre Francais, under the management of

---

[114] Of this renowned Bergamosque the story is told that, while he was
convulsing with laughter the crowds that were attracted by his extraordinary comic humour, he was himself a prey to an unconquerable melancholy ;
and that, consulting an eminent physician upon his malady, he was recommended to try the effect of witnessing the performances of Carlin, of which
all Paris " rung from side to side." " Alas ! sir," said the unhappy
patient, " you see the miserable Carlin before you." The story, whether
true or false, has been thought good enough to carry double, at least. It
has been told of our English Aristophanes, Samuel Foote, and I believe
also of Liston.

[115] The very pretty entertainment of *Les deux Edmons* was highly
relished by the Londoners, during the successful career of the company of
French actors at the Tottenham Street Theatre (1822 to 1826). Laporte
and the late unfortunate Pélissié were admirable in the two principal characters.

Picard,[116] the celebrated dramatic author, had recently established itself in the Feydeau, in consequence of the destructive
fire at the Odéon. Notwithstanding the assistance of the manager's very clever and very numerous comedies, it had but a
languishing existence. Attracted by the title, I was present
at the performance of the play of *Tom Jones*, which was certainly amusing enough, rather from its absurdities and ridiculous contrasts with the great original, than from its own
merits. Picard himself played the part of Squire Western, or,
as they spelled it, Westiern.

Of the numerous small theatres on the Boulevards, that of
the Ambigu Comique was then most in vogue. *Pièces à grand
spectacle*, melodramas, and broad farce, constituted the attractions which drew nightly to this theatre crowds of spectators
of a class not the most refined. The chief actor, manager, and
proprietor, Corse, displayed a good deal of coarse humour in
his performance. So much for the Parisian playhouses : the
Opéra Italien was not open at this period of the year.

I had only one opportunity of being enabled to form an
opinion of the eloquence of the French bar, in attending a trial
at the law courts—the Palais de Justice. The subject was a
disputed claim of property, of great amount, but of no general
interest. The pleadings were, however, highly animated, and
gave a very favourable idea of their forensic oratory. The
court had nothing very imposing in its appearance, or its forms
of proceeding, but the strictest order and decorum prevailed.
There were three judges on the bench, with but little distinc-

---

[116] Picard's works are voluminous, and of very unequal merits. His
very pretty comedies of *La Petite Ville* and *Les Ricochets* are well known
to the visiters of the French theatre in London, 1823-4. He was a pains-
taking but very indifferent actor, in his own company of comedians.

tion in their costume ; and the counsel were attired in a simple
suit of black. The wig, that venerable appendage to our judi-
cature, was wanting altogether, so that the wisdom of the tri-
bunal, whatever it might be, could not be libelled, as in England, by being attributed to that respectable decoration. The
principal counsel, whose name I have forgotten, argued with
great clearness, fluency, and choice of expression, and reminded
me of our own celebrated Garrow more than of any other person
to whom I could compare him. I would remark that a better
school of study for the language could not be found than that
which is afforded by the Parisian law-courts. Indeed, the difference between the French spoken by the educated classes
in the metropolis and that which is heard every where else
is too evident to pass unnoticed by even the least discrimi-
nating.

It would be scarcely fair to judge of pulpit oratory in France
by what was at this period to be found in Paris. The expa-
triation of the priests and the atheistical doctrines of the revolution had left but few preachers, even had there been hearers
pious enough or bold enough to listen to them ; but certainly,
from the few specimens that came under my notice, I should
say that the cause of religion derived but little support from
the eloquence of the clergy. A better state of things was
believed to be approaching ; and among the benefits supposed
to have been conferred on the nation by Bonaparte was that
of the re-establishment of the worship of their fathers. The
Sunday in France was, however, but little distinguishable by
observances from every other day, except as to its greater air
of gaiety, and the general devotion of the people to amusement.
A great many of the shops and all the theatres and places of
public entertainment were open, and the latter were more fre-

quented than at any other time, though not by the upper
classes. The usages of France and England are in many points
in striking contrast with each other, but in none more so, perhaps, than in the appearance that Sunday exhibits in the
respective countries.   The aspect of London, with all the
shops rigidly closed, the streets deserted, and the awful, pal-
pable, and universal stillness that prevails, with scarcely a
living creature to be seen, conveys a feeling of horror to the
Frenchman, as if he were suddenly transported to a city of the
dead ; while the Englishman in Paris, even though not what
has been called strait-laced in his notions, does not easily reconcile himself to that outrage upon all his early habits which
the unbounded license of the French Sunday presents.   Cards,
billiards, draughts, and dominoes, are constantly played, even
by those who, in passing a few minutes in a church at seven
o'clock in the morning, think they have acquitted themselves
of their religious duties, and are at full liberty, for the rest of
the day, to enjoy themselves according to their inclinations.
It must be confessed that the spirit, hilarity, and *abandon*,
with which the French enter upon even the most trivial
amusements is exhilarating to look upon.

The environs of Paris are not to be compared, I think, for
beauty of various kinds, with those of London.   The views
from St.-Cloud, for instance, are decidedly inferior to those
from Richmond and Hampstead ; and Versailles,[117] with all

[117] A French nobleman, who expressed himself enraptured with the
beauty of a palace and gardens in a foreign country, was asked in the
midst of his admiration how they stood, in his opinion, compared with those
of Versailles.   " Ah, parbleu ! Monsieur," said he, " Versailles était fait
exprès pour n'être comparé à rien."   An elegant rebuke to the questioner,
in declining to make a comparison, which is proverbially odious.

its magnificence, is but the creation of art alone ; while Windsor
and Greenwich superadd to their splendid buildings unequalled charms of natural situation, that are quite beyond the
reach of any imitative power. St.-Cloud, from its elevation
and its vicinity to the capital, affords a good view of Paris,
and its elegant palace and the rural character of its park are
exceedingly interesting and agreeable, though the finest prospect that I have seen near the metropolis is that from the terrace of St.-Germain. The lofty, but heavy, brick palace, in
which our unhappy James the Second passed the latter years
of his life, and its present desolate appearance, excite melancholy reflections, and contribute to the gloomy and deserted
look of the place altogether. I was rather fortunate in the
opportunity of visiting Versailles under favourable circumstances. The splendid waterworks, which constitute the
greatest wonder of the gardens, were exhibited for the first
time since the revolution—a period of thirteen or fourteen
years ; and the announcement had, as may be readily imagined,
excited the highest interest among both the residents and
visiters of Paris. I believe it is only on extraordinary occasions that the grand display of the fountains takes place at any
period, being attended each time with considerable expense—
several hundred pounds, as I was given to understand. Without vainly attempting a description of that which I am per-
suaded no words could adequately describe, I will merely
observe that the whole scene—the flashing and glittering of
innumerable *jets d'eau* in myriads of sparkles bright as dia-
monds, under the influence of a glowing sun in August, pouring
its flood of light from a sky without a cloud, and witnessed as
from a natural and verdant amphitheatre by more than 200,000
people (as estimated), a large proportion of the immense throng

females in gay attire, mostly without bonnets ; the whole scene, the striking effect of this brilliant spectacle, left an impression on my mind that will never be effaced from my recollection.

Versailles may justly be considered as the triumph of art : the palace and gardens are the very *acmé* of its power ; but however admirable and imposing may be the objects, still the artificial grandeur of mere human workmanship will always want something of the charm produced by a judicious adaptation and union of nature and art. In the Grand and in the Petit-Trianon, the predominance of the artificial character is equally obvious ; and in the Petit-Trianon especially, the little dairy, the little lake, the little ship, the little observatory, and the many other littlenesses, became trifling and toylike in the childishness of their imitation.[118]

The palace of Versailles, though not inhabited since 1792, was still in nearly the same state as when the residence of the ill-fated Louis XVI. and Marie Antoinette. The long range of splendid apartments, gorgeously furnished and decorated with numerous pictures by French masters, many of them of great excellence, were thrown open on this occasion to the public. There was too little time allowed to admit of any thing like an accurate examination, but I was greatly struck with the exquisite beauty of the drawing-rooms, the state bed-

[118] The Petit-Trianon was the peculiarly favoured retreat of the young and lovely Marie Antoinette. Its present state of desolation, its unfurnished apartments, and the deathlike stillness which prevails — the etiquette of the official, who uncovers as he conducts visiters through the apartments, together with the spontaneous respect of strangers to the sacredness of a place consecrated by the unparalleled misfortunes of its royal owners—all contribute to excite reflections of the most painful interest.

room, the chapel, and the theatre.[119]   The hall in which was
given the entertainment to the officers of the royal guards, and
at which their enthusiasm was excited to the utmost by the
unexpected appearance of the royal family among them, was an
object of great interest from the melancholy associations connected with it.   Indeed, it was impossible to traverse these
apartments, within so few years the site of the splendid entertainments of the most brilliant court of Europe, with a queen
beaming in youthful beauty, without, at the same time, feeling
the most poignant regret and commiseration for the sufferings
that both she and the unhappy Louis were doomed to undergo[120] from the atrocious cruelty of their savage perse-
cutors.

Paris, though much less commodious, cleanly, or comfortable than London, as a metropolis for the residence of a large
population, is, what may be termed, more picturesque, and
abounds with public buildings of striking beauty and effect.
The Louvre and its incomparable façade, the Invalides, S^te.
Genevieve, and many other noble works of architecture, will
fully justify the claim of the French to great distinction in this

[119] The St. James's Theatre is an exact imitation — rather on a larger
scale — of the theatre in the palace of Versailles.

[120] After an interval of twenty-three years, I again saw, in 1825, the
gardens and exterior of the palace of Versailles.   " It was a sorry sight."
The palace closely shut up, the gardens neglected, with scarcely a living
being to be seen but the few soldiers acting as guards or police—the
statues, lakes, terraces, marble flights of steps, in short, all the glories of
days gone by, bearing sad evidence of the vanity of human power.   It has
recently (1837) been set in order, and prepared as a national historical
picture-gallery by command of Louis-Philippe, and to be open to the
public under certain regulations.

branch of art.[121] The view from the Quai Voltaire on the south bank of the Seine is eminently beautiful; and though the river, being but a narrow stream, especiallyin the dry season, compared with our majestic Thames does not of itself make an imposing object, the spacious quays and terraces on its banks, with the palaces and gardens in its vicinity, form an *ensemble* that surpasses any thing of the kind that can be seen at London. The Château, as it is called, of the Tuileries, is a grand but somewhat heavy-looking structure; but the gardens, with the Place de la Concorde, and the Champs-Elysées, are said by the French, and perhaps with reason, to be unequalled in the *coup d'œil* as an entrance by any capital in Europe.

The public promenades are thronged on fine summer evenings with company made up of all classes, wishing to see and to be seen; a disposition which the French seem to enjoy in a superlative degree. The Palais-Royal and the Boulevards are frequented at a later hour and by less respectable society than are the gardens of the Tuileries and the Luxembourg, and animated by a joyous spirit, that might perhaps degenerate into disorder, but for the vigilant superintendence of the police. Taking but a superficial view, foreigners are disposed to consider that Englishmen make a pleasure of business, and a business of pleasure; that we engage in each, with much the same serious aspect; and enjoy our diversions with an earnest gravity similar to that with which we enter upon most important undertakings. Frenchmen plunge into what they deem amusement (however trivial it may be thought by others) with a

---

[121] The more recent productions of the French architects, namely, the Bourse, La Madelaine, and L'Arc de l'Étoile, well sustain the national reputation.

laisser aller and apparent relish peculiar to their nation. This susceptibility of enjoyment on the one hand, and their buoyancy of spirit in adversity on the other, seem to make the French elasticity of character the most enviable in existence, as it would scarcely be fair to impute their firmness in misfortune to insensibility, while we admit them to be so quick in their feelings of pleasurable impressions. If singing and dancing are emanations of cheerfulness, the French have irrefragable claims to the title of a happy people, as the song and the dance, particularly the latter, are in requisition at every assemblage, from the *soirée bourgeoise* to the *guinguette* and the village green.[122]

The English who in 1802 visited Paris in such shoals, had no reason to complain of their reception by the French, though some fears had been entertained that the remains of the Jacobinical spirit, combined with the irritation excited against England by the late war, might have rendered it any thing but flattering. The horror felt by the French at the recollection of the executions and massacres of 1792-1793 and 1794 made the way comparatively easy for the establishment of a military despotism—the ordinary result of a previous state of anarchy. Few vestiges were to be seen of the revolutionary hurricane that had passed over the land, and the manners

[122] The passion for dancing in France, and the little taste shewn for it in England, strongly marks one of the many points of distinction between the habits of two nations who are such near neighbours of each other. A foreign friend, when visiting London, was informed by his French *valet de place* that he (the valet) had been five years in this country, and had never once, during the whole of that time, seen an instance of the people dancing. My friend mentioned this information to me with such an air of mingled surprise, incredulity, and disdain, that I did not feel disposed to confirm the account by my own experience to the same effect for all the years I had lived, but simply admitted that it was possible.

of the people seemed gradually sobering down to the usual
French urbanity.   Beyond the occasional use (and that very
rarely, and never but by the labouring classes) of the republican
term *Citoyen* instead of Monsieur, with the universally worn
tricoloured cockade about the size of a shilling, and the words
"*dix d'Août*" painted in white letters on the walls of the Tuileries where the cannon-balls had struck on that dreadful day,
there was little to remind a stranger of recent events.   The
Milor of the old *régime* was even now and then addressed
to an Englishman by some sycophant rogue, who thought he
might gain his object, whatever it might happen to be, by a
little flattery of John Bull.[123]

There is an obvious advantage in favour of the inhabitant of
a dear country, who sojourns in one comparatively cheap.
Almost every thing in England that requires a shilling for its
purchase may be obtained in France for a franc (ten-pence) or
less.   Thus at once here is a bounty of more than 16 per cent.
enabling the Englishman in the very outset to make £500 go
as far, as the phrase is, in France as £600 in England.   But
the pecuniary advantage is certainly much greater than this,
and would not be over-stated perhaps, in naming 25 or 30 per
cent.   That such a temptation, coupled with those of a more

[123] At an after-period, an evident change took place in the feelings of
Frenchmen towards England. I had opportunities of observing, in 1824
and 1825, that there was much less amenity in the demeanour of the Parisians towards their English visiters than I had witnessed in 1802. The
battle of Waterloo can scarcely be forgiven, though the French have probably been great gainers by it; still the immense sums expended by the
English must always insure them civil treatment. By a calculation founded
upon official documents, it appears that the annual expenditure of English
residents and travellers in France amounts to more than four millions
sterling, at a moderate computation.

genial climate, facilities of economizing, and the various *agrémens*
that are afforded by a residence in France, should cause a numerous list of absentees, is not to be wondered at, however it
may be regretted.   One recollection connected with this subject
and with the season I passed in Paris is strongly impressed on
my memory ; namely, the profusion of delicious fruit at a very
low price, such as peaches and grapes of excellent quality, at
less than a fifth of what they would cost in London.[124]   Certainly the comforts of (literally) our firesides, and many others
that have become from habit almost identified with an Englishman's existence, are not to be met with in France ; which, together with a pretty general though vague notion of the insta-
bility of the government, will counteract the tendencies of our
countrymen to a permanent domiciliation there, notwithstanding
the comparative cheap living.   The inducements that have influenced so many parents to send their children to France in
the hope of obtaining an education for them at a moderate expense, and of their acquiring at the same time the language,
now considered indispensable, are, I am inclined to think,
somewhat fallacious.   A youth necessarily imbibes the notions,
more or less, of those with whom he is associated ; and what
can compensate for the loss of his distinctive character as an
Englishman ?—a character, in spite of its imputed degeneracy,
respected by all the world, and always able to command respect,
which character, perhaps, is to be preserved only by a truly
English education.   Admitting that a facility of talking French
may be gained by a young person remaining a few years in the
country, it is invariably at the sacrifice of something of their

[124] Butcher's meat, poultry, bread, and vegetables, are all much cheaper
in France than with us.   It may be difficult, under the mystification of
French cookery, to discover the genuine flavour of what is brought to table ;

native tongue. Every language has its own peculiar *chant* or recitative, and English, if not altogether lost by a lengthened residence in France, is sure to be infected with an accent that is foreign, disagreeable, and difficult, if not impossible to get rid of. Neither should the probability of a change of religion be disregarded where the duty of proselytism is so earnestly fulfilled as it is by the Roman Catholic priesthood.

One of the most striking differences in the habits of the people in France and in England, is the greater temperance and sobriety of the former—the more to be admired as the means of intoxication are easily obtained. Even in good company, the English practice, "more honoured in the breach than in the observance," does not prevail, of setting in to a drinking-bout after dinner, and after driving the ladies to their drawing-room. This has been justly urged against us as a reproach to our taste, in thus depriving ourselves of the charm of female society, when it would be most amiable and exhilarating. The first clause of the censure may be said scarcely to apply of late years, as we are becoming a more sober nation;[125] but we still adhere to the bowing out the ladies after drenching them with a glass of wine. Something however must be allowed for the inherent differences in the respective character and destina-

but I have eaten excellent roast beef, rump-steak, &c. in Paris. To be sure, it was at the house of an English friend, and dressed by an English cook. The bread, poultry, and vegetables are unexceptionable; sea-fish, from the distance it must necessarily be carried, is at a high price and not remarkably fresh; milk and butter very good; beer not very good; and wine and brandy, as all the world knows, that needs no bush.

[125] Our habits of excess had been "reformed indifferently," even before the establishment of Temperance Societies: now, it is to be presumed, we shall "reform them altogether."

tions of English and of French women. The principal object of
the French woman, from fifteen to fourscore, is by the display of
her wit and accomplishments to attract the admiration of the
other sex. This is by no means limited to those who happen
to be gifted by nature with beauty of person, or superiority of
intellect, but extends equally to the old and young, the handsome or ugly, the silly or sensible. The men, on their part,
foster this disposition for purposes of their own, by the most
heartless and extravagant adulation. Women in France are
prominently occupied in business, negociation, and political in-
trigue. The most important duties connected with "man's
best delight, well-order'd home," are but slightly attended to ;
the matrimonial yoke hangs loosely ; the children are sent to
nurse ; Monsieur dines at a restaurateur's, and Madame is left
at liberty to amuse herself as she thinks fit.[126]

As if the taste, manners, and customs must, as it were, of
necessity, be strongly opposed in the two countries, it would
be difficult to name any subject in which a marked contra-
riety did not exist, and in which the superiority would not be
claimed by a true Frenchman for his own.[127] Their houses
are lofty—six or seven stories high ; their rooms large ; each
floor usually occupied by a separate family ; the staircase and

[126] Marriage and concubinage bear a very different bearing and proportion to each other in France and in England, as is evinced by the fact
officially given in the statistical reports, of nearly one-third of the number of children born in Paris being of unmarried parents. We are yet, in
this country, a good way off this degree of ultra-liberalism.

[127] An amusing instance of pertinacious nationality is cited by Sir Walter Scott, in *Paul's Letters to his Kinsfolk*, wherein, to the supposed
unassailable advantages of the English flagged pavement for foot-passen-
gers, the Frenchman retorts that "it may be very well for Messieurs les
Anglais, but, for his part, he prefers *la totalité de la rue !*"

other conveniences common to all, and rendered by neglect and
filth an utter abomination ; the comforts of carpets, rugs, and
floorcloths, almost unknown ; apartments richly furnished for
purposes of parade, and those for the ordinary domestic service
incongruously and inadequately supplied, while there is a too
evident and universal want of that tidiness that forms so striking and so agreeable a feature in English housewifery. Our
superiority in this respect being too manifest to be denied, the
French, as I had occasion to remark more than once, console
themselves (never being at a loss for something to say, even in
the most desperate cases) by quoting the Dutch, a nation they
hold in great contempt, as at least our equals in this very trivial
quality.   But in France, palaces, churches, gardens, &c., exhibit everywhere a deficiency of that predominating spirit of
care and good order which gives an additional charm to beauty
of every kind, and often compensates for the want of it ; while
the senses are frequently shocked by the most incongruous
union or neighbourhood of filth and finery, magnificence and
meanness.[128] The French are a fine race of men, but, from the
neglect of a uniform attention to their personal appearance, do
not generally show to advantage. The anomaly of a clean
shirt, with an unshaven beard, a phenomenon unknown in
Britain, is of no uncommon occurrence in France.   Sterne in
his *Sentimental Journey* remarks, that there is a larger proportion of crooked and deformed persons observable in Paris

[128] Refuse of all kinds, decayed vegetables, &c., are thrown into the
streets, and, notwithstanding the exertions of the scavengers, early in the
morning, to remove them and other nuisances, the contamination is still
perceptible in the air of many parts of the town. There is very little un-
derground sewerage in Paris, and no water laid on to each house, as in
London.

than elsewhere. I think that the average equality of well-looking men is less than in London : that there are more very tall, very short, very fat, and very thin people to be met with in Paris, in proportion to the population, than with us ; but I am also disposed to believe that in a given number of individuals full as many favourable specimens of the " human *form* divine " might be found among our neighbours as we could produce at home. The superior beauty of English women is universally acknowledged ; though a great drawback is made on account of the awkward, heavy, and ungainly demeanour[129] of our ladies, when contrasted with the elegance of the French *tournure*. This *tournure*, on which the French women plume themselves so much, and not without reason, is a graceful, unembarrassed deportment, entirely free from all that constraint and *mauvaise honte* which is supposed peculiarly to belong to the English character. On the other hand, this vaunted elegance has been attributed to the mere practice of picking their way through the muddy streets of Paris, in which the French females show extraordinary cleverness.

The tone of good society seems altogether on a much more agreeable and familiar footing in France than it is in England ; less encumbered with formality and etiquette ; and where the solemn pause, the dead silence, and overpowering *ennui* that are sometimes encountered in an English drawing-room are utterly unknown. The French ladies are here in their element, and appear to great advantage.[130] In addition to the

---

[129] The opportunities afforded to the spirit of imitation, in a two-and-twenty years' friendly intercourse between the two nations, has partly removed this stigma ; it is to be hoped that no grounds for more serious reproach have been substituted.

[130] Men and women, by their different habits of life in England, are

charms of their manner and address, they have great powers of conversation, both in *matériel* and in mode of expression— never sinking to the inanity and nothingness of mere cap and bonnet talk, and, with equal good sense and good taste, avoiding all approach to the recondite and profound disquisitions of blue-stocking philosophy. The admirable letters of Madame de Sévigné, Madame du Deffand, &c., and the works of Madame de Graffigny, Madame de Genlis, Madame Cottin, and many others that might be named, prove with what consummate ability they cultivate their appropriate class of literature.

The manners of the people generally, without being rude or insolent, were, at this period (1802), somewhat abrupt and familiar, differing greatly, I should suppose, from the gentle and conciliatory character of the French in by-gone times. Still an Englishman had abundant cause to be satisfied with his reception in Paris, notwithstanding the recent hostilities between the two countries might have left some embittered feelings. But political affairs were now in a position that gratified the national vanity, and put them in good humour with all the world. Jacobinism had been completely put down by the ascendency of Bonaparte ; and with his supreme power and military despotism the people were well reconciled, as they were relieved thereby from the horrors and agitations of the revolution. It did not quite accord with an Englishman's notions to find, in any situation, the soldiery mixed up in

necessarily less in company with each other than they are in France. Few females, comparatively, with us, are engaged in business ; and our system of clubs and public dinners, carried to such an extent as it now is, must tend still more and more to this result. It may, however, have its advantages.

rather large proportions with the rest of the population, and
constantly on duty at every public place of amusement. The
blaze of republicanism had been pretty well trodden down,
though occasional sparks were sometimes elicited, more especially in contact with the " unwashed." There was, as might be
expected, a little more than the usual professional *hauteur* to
be seen in the demeanour of the military ; but this was a trifle
in the exchange of a mob-government, for one of order and
tranquillity. Voltaire, in one of his letters, observes that he
would rather live under the despotism of a single *lion* than
under that of two or three hundred *rats* like himself. Without
disputing the reasonableness of his sentiment, it may still be
admitted that tyranny in any form must necessarily check the
development of the mind and faculties of man, at the same
time that it fetters his civil, political, and religious liberty.
The visible sign of this oppressive power that, at this period,
was most ostensibly displayed, and most strongly revolted the
feelings of the English visiters, was the universal appearance
of a military detachment at every place of public amusement,
both withinside and without.   Indeed, the police of Paris
seemed generally to be in the hands of the soldiery ; and
though the duties were allowed to be executed with gentleness,
and even forbearance, yet it was somewhat startling, particularly at night, to meet at every turn patrols of various different regiments, both horse and foot.   As far as my own observation enabled me to judge, I would say that the military
constituted the most urbane and civilized class of the community.   I never had occasion to make an inquiry of a sentinel,
without receiving either the fullest information, or directions that
put me in the way to obtain it, and was invariably addressed
by them as *monsieur*, not *citoyen*, and in terms of politeness

and intelligence that would seldom be met with in the same class in England.

The foregoing, slight, and very imperfect observations during a two months' visit to Paris, in 1802, were made at the moment, and have no pretension beyond that of being equally unpremeditated and sincere. The incidents of this short period form some of the most agreeable of my recollections, and contributed greatly to raise the French character in my estimation above the prejudices almost universally entertained in England upon the subject. This favourable opinion has been abundantly confirmed on subsequent occasions; and with respect to that class, more especially, with which professional pursuits made me most acquainted, it is with equal pride and pleasure that I record my humble tribute of acknowledgment to the candour, liberality, and friendliness of the artists of France.

By way of varying the scene, I returned to England by the Picardy road, through Amiens, Abbeville, Montreuil, &c:; but this part of France is, with little exception, extremely dull and uninteresting. The Cathedral at Amiens is, however, a noble specimen of gothic architecture, which would form a striking object in any situation; but the effect of which is in this instance enhanced by the flat, monotonous character of the surrounding country. I had little time to indulge my admiration, as the diligence waited but to change horses; though the silence and stillness of the streets, together with the freshness and beauty of a September morning, at sun-rise, no doubt contributed in some degree to the impression made upon me by the whole scene. Abbeville, in its pleasant valley, and Montreuil, on its elevation, are both agreeably situated towns, and well worth a longer notice than can be given by a passing traveller.

Boulogne, where the passengers by our slow conveyance breakfasted the second morning after that of our departure from
Paris, was then a mere French sea-coast town, peopled by
merchants, traders, smugglers, and fishermen. It has since
become a favoured retreat for the English of all ranks and
stations, from the peer to the pickpocket : a bathing-place for
the Londoners in summer, and a city of refuge at all seasons for
the broken-down gentleman, whose means have failed him, and
for the fraudulent debtor and the desperate adventurer whose
means have *availed* them. At one of the few shops that were
open at the very early hour we passed through, I inquired of
the tradesman, in making some trifling purchase, whether the
attack of Nelson, in 1800, had excited great terror in the
town. He replied with characteristic *nonchalance*, "that it
caused but little sensation, inasmuch as the inhabitants felt
perfectly confident in their means of defence," a feeling which
the event fully justified.

We at length arrived at Calais, after being more than fifty
hours boxed-up in the diligence—no small penance on ordinary
occasions ; but, as it happened fortunately that our fellow-
travellers were three British officers of the 13th, returning
from Egypt (Major Weller, Captain Belford, and Lieutenant Blake), whose manners, intelligence, and good-temper
smoothed all difficulties, our journey became a real party of
pleasure.

Calais has somewhat of the appearance of an English town ;
and here, at an excellent hotel, Ducroz's Lion d'Argent, we
passed a delightful day, rendered doubly so by the gay spirits
and companionable qualities of our military friends, and the
anticipation of a speedy landing in old England. At the
bureau, where we attended for the examination of our pass-

ports, and which was presided over by Mengaud, a well-known revolutionist, I felt not a little indignant at perceiving, in addition to the general tone of official arrogance, the walls of an ante-room in which we waited were decorated with the masterly caricatures of Gillray, ridiculing the chief personages of the English administration—Lord Hawkesbury, Mr. Addington, and others. The haughty insolence of demeanour assumed towards our countrymen by all the small fry of hangers-on to the consular government indicated, too plainly to be mistaken, the unfriendly feeling that prevailed in higher quarters, and which was so soon made manifest in the renewal of hostilities. The truce (for it was nothing else) of Amiens was, I suppose, proper and judicious as an experiment ; but it was evident that, as the *game* had not been played out between the contending parties, no lasting peace could yet be looked for. The boatmen who landed us on the beach at Dover seemed to feel deeply the humiliation of being obliged to submit to the great change that had taken place in their concerns, the Frenchmen being now allowed, as they stated it, to have their own way altogether. As soon as our party jumped on shore, we gave three cheers that, in the stillness of the night, reverberated among the cliffs, and were distinctly heard, as we were told the next day, within the walls of the castle. This expression of gladness, at the return to one's native land—a land, too, of order, freedom, and security—was, at this period, of frequent occurrence. We had an opportunity, the following morning, of viewing the fortifications, accompanied by our *compagnons de voyage*, who had friends in the garrison ; and, having taken places in the night-coach, arrived in London after an absence of two months, passed so delightfully that the mere recollection has ever since been to me a source of enjoyment. I had the pleasure of meeting our friendly fellow-travellers[131] once, and but once, afterwards in town. They departed almost immediately to join their respective families, and I doggedly resumed my professional labours, though it certainly required a resolute and persevering effort on my part to pursue my studies with due attention, after such an interval so differently employed.

The money I had received for engraving three of the *Arabian Nights'* plates (about £70) not only enabled me to make the excursion to Paris, but, small as the sum was, encouraged me to enter into a sort of joint-stock speculation with Miller, the publisher, and the Reverend Mr. Forster, the editor of the *Arabian Nights*, which turned out badly for me. This was an edition, in quarto, of *Rasselas*, to which, for my share in the concern, I was to supply the engravings, five in number, the clergyman and the bookseller to provide the pictures by Smirke, the letter-press, &c. I do not like to dwell on this subject, as I have great reason to believe that I was made the dupe and victim of an unprincipled scheme. However, by the usual kind assistance at home, which was never withheld, I

[131] Major Weller, become Lieutenant-Colonel, died in the year 1837, in Ireland, as I saw noticed in the newspaper. Of Captain Belford, who was a married man, and Lieutenant Blake, of the Blakes of Galway, I have never since heard. Blake was commissioned by Mr. Fagan, consul at Naples, with some of the smaller curiosities dug out of Pompeii, to be delivered personally to the Prince of Wales. Blake showed them to me as a matter of great favour. They were in perfect preservation and exquisitely beautiful. Blake had, of course, a most gracious reception by the Prince, and was quite enchanted with his affability and elegant manners. Fagan was an Englishman, and had been a pupil of Bartolozzi; and, some years after this period, committed suicide by throwing himself from a window at Rome.

weathered this check without any material injury ; and as a
powerful impulse had been now given to the decoration, in a
superior way, of the standard literature of the country, I had
the prospect of sufficient occupation in engraving to warrant
my discarding altogether as a profession miniature and portrait
painting, which at one period I was disposed to adopt, but
which I was soon convinced could not be carried on with another pursuit advantageously to either. I had painted in my
early time a good many miniatures, and had drawn a number
of portraits in coloured chalks, and was about making the experiment of painting in oil, to which end I made some studies at
the Royal Academy, with the brush and two or three colours ;
but commissions now became so frequent that my whole time
was assiduously engaged, whilst the retirement and independence of spirit that may accompany the practice of engraving,
with the public at large for a patron, were more congenial to
my disposition. This is, perhaps, the only circumstance that
can be named in its favour, in comparison with various other
branches of the fine arts ; the slowness of its process and
the difficulty of its acquirement, together with the very inadequate remuneration for unequalled toil and seclusion, without even the chance of a good prize in the lottery of professional
life, rendering the smallest possible return for the greatest personal sacrifices. The increased taste or fashion for highly-em-
bellished books naturally led to more active competition among
the caterers for the public ; and the names of Du Roveray[132]

---

[132] Du Roveray was a merchant, or stockbroker, and by way of amusement, I suppose, occupied his leisure in publishing handsome editions of
Pope, Gray, &c., exceedingly well embellished, but by which it may be
doubted whether he obtained much profit, though he certainly proved
himself possessed of some taste. He afterwards became a collector and

and Sharpe[133] may be cited as among the most active
speculators in ornamental literature, who now sought the
aid of the engravers in their several projects. The first-
named was an amateur publisher, and for him I executed
nothing. Sharpe is known by his embellished edition of the
Spectator, &c., &c., in which most of the engravers of the
Arabian Nights were engaged, myself among them. Eighteen
guineas were paid for each plate, and this sum was thought a
liberal price at this time; and so it certainly was in comparison to the six or seven guineas which Cooke had dealt out for
his edition of the poets a few years before. The impulse now
given by the encouragement of the public brought, of course,
other publishers into the field of competition, among whom
may be named Messrs. Longman,[134] Cadell, Suttaby, Kears-

dealer in drawings and pictures, in a small way, and is, I believe, (1839)
still living. He was an old bachelor, and of rather singular appearance,
wearing his hair powdered and plaited in a long tail, doubled and fastened
by a comb on the top of his head. He was a small man, and was accustomed to ride from the city to the west-end upon a large horse, of which
he seemed somewhat proud.

[133] John Sharpe, publisher of an ornamented edition of the *Spectator,
Tatler,* and *Guardian,* well known as a perfectly honest and honourable
man in all his dealings, has not obtained the success in life that he has so
well deserved: proving, if it needed proof, that integrity, cleverness, industry, and perseverance, do not always ensure a prosperous result. In
1803, I accompanied him on a visit to his relations in Cambridge and
Bury St. Edmonds. He is now living (1839) at Kensington.

[134] Longman and Co. This old established and extensive house of
business is too well known to render any particular notice at all necessary.
Embellished books form but a small item in their immense concern; as may
also be said of that of Cadell and Davis—whose *Don Quixote,* with 74
engravings from pictures by Smirke, is, perhaps, unique of its kind. Sut-

ley, and Miller. To the liberal dealing of every one of these gentlemen I can, and do, with great pleasure, bear the fullest testimony, as far as regards myself; and the higher prices paid to engravers, from the increased demand for decorated books, was a necessary result. The highest prices, however, need but to be named to prove that there are no great pecuniary advantages attending the difficult and laborious practice of this ingenious, elegant, and useful art; and, for other inducements to its pursuit, it would not be easy to find any, unless, as I have already observed, in its independence of all patronage but that of the public, and its facilities of extensive diffusion.

About this period, (1806) the Rev. E. Forster, in union with Miller, the bookseller, started with a scheme of a series of plates, from the old masters chiefly, under the title of the *British Gallery of Engravings*, which, like most other works of a similar kind, "drew its slow length along" for some years, and then was seen no more. Another publication from Longman's house, with coloured prints by Tomkins and others, made its appearance also about the same time, in competition with Forster's, with the name of *British Gallery of Pictures*,

taby's elegant miniature editions of the poets, with their combined claims of printing and decoration, had great success. Every plate was occupied by two subjects, one of them a small vignette, and I received for each of mine twenty-five guineas, and fourteen guineas in addition for reparations during the printing of 6000 or 7000 impressions. Mr. Suttaby, one of the very best of good men, died in 1838. Kearsley, of Fleet Street, was unsuccessful in business. The *Gil Blas*, from Smirke's pictures, was projected and commenced by him, and afterwards sold to and published by Longman and Co. Miller, of Albemarle Street, retired with a competency early in life. He was a man of rather stiff manners, which led to his receiving from Constable, of Edinburgh, the sobriquet of Lord Albemarle, which he always retained.

which had also an unsuccessful result, ending in a public lottery of the stock and materials. I engraved several for Forster's work, among which was Sir Joshua Reynolds's Ugolino
and his Sons, from a copy painted by Howard, and for which
I received one hundred and sixty guineas. About this time
I also executed a plate of Nelson, when a lieutenant, about to
board an American prize, for the *Life of Nelson* by the Rev.
Stanier Clarke,[135] (elder brother of the traveller, Dr. Clarke)
and Mr. McArthur.

In 1804, in company with my early and constant friend,
Mr. Emmerson, I visited the west of England, Bath, Bristol,
and Glastonbury. In the early part of the year 1805 I married ; and at the latter end of the same year I lost my respected
father,[136] who, with the full concurrence and wishes of his
children, bequeathed the whole of his property to his widow,

[135] The Rev. Stanier Clarke had an appointment in the Prince of Wales's
household.

[136] My father died at Hendon, on the 16th of December, 1805, and my
mother in London, January the 27th, 1807. A gravestone to each marks
the spot where they lie in the churchyard of the pretty and secluded village
of Hendon. Mr. Hayley, the poet, very kindly wrote a few lines at my
request, which are inscribed on their tombs. In the autumn of 1807, on
the invitation of Mr. Hayley, I passed a few days at his delightful retreat
at Felpham, by the sea-side, near Bognor, and continued in correspondence
with him for some years, till his ill-assorted match with a wife forty years
younger than himself. This was his second marriage, and, like his first,
turned out badly. His villa was an elegant retirement, and was redolent
of Cowper, Romney, and Flaxman, Charlotte Smith and Anna Seward.
While I was there, two or three persons " whose names are not unknown
to fame " called at the Hermitage, as he was pleased to designate his residence: Mr. Huskisson, Mr. Sargent, M. P. (the author of a poem called
The Mine) Lady Sudley, &c. I afterwards corresponded with him till his
above-mentioned marriage with Miss Wellsford, of Blackheath.

my mother. I mention this as a testimony of the implicit
and affectionate confidence deservedly borne to this exemplary
woman by those who were enabled most justly to love and
appreciate her kind and gentle and disinterested devotedness
to their welfare. She survived my father only thirteen months,
dying at the age of sixty-five, on the 27th of January, 1807.
This was the heaviest affliction, with one sad, sad exception,
that ever befel me. That exception was the death, about nine
years afterwards, of my first-born, my most beloved daughter,
Julia Elizabeth, at the age of ten years and two months. She
was buried at Hendon, in the same grave with my mother.

> —— O! what a world were this,
> How unendurable its weight, if they
> Whom Death hath sunder'd did not meet again!
> SOUTHEY.

But

> —— favour'd in their lot are they
> Who are not left to learn below
> That length of life is length of woe.
> SOUTHEY.

On my marriage, my father generously presented me with
one of his houses in Warren Street, Fitzroy Square, and, far-
ther, enabled me to fit it up in a respectable and commodious
way for the exercise of my profession. In this house all my
children were born, and the chief portion of my artistical
labours produced. I resided in it uninterruptedly for twenty-
six years and more, (from the spring of 1805 to the autumn of
1831) when I removed with my family to a pleasant residence
at Greenwich, overlooking the Park on the south side, and the
river and its ever-moving panorama of ships and boats on the
other.

I have now to bring forward the name of an individual who,

both as an artist and a man, is an honour to his country—
David Wilkie; with whom I first became personally acquainted
in the year 1807, when he lived in the Hampstead Road. I had
still continued fully occupied with engagements with various
booksellers, when the great success of Burnet's print from Wilkie's admirable picture of the Blind Fiddler, and some dissatisfaction between the parties, led to his proposing to me in 1812
a joint-stock adventure, in which we should be the sole proprietors, he finding the picture and I the engraving. Anxious as
I had long been for an opportunity of trying my hand upon a
larger scale than I had been accustomed to, and thereby obtaining at least a chance of escape from the thraldom of devoting
the labours of a whole life to the end, as it would seem, of their
being shut up in a book, I gladly and at once acceded to the
proposition. The mutual conditions of our engagement were
promptly arranged upon the basis, with various modifications,
of one-third share to Wilkie, and two-thirds to me; which
terms were afterwards changed to one-fourth and three-fourths
respectively, at the generous and unsolicited suggestion of
Wilkie, who considered the first adopted proportions as bearing
rather hard upon me, and throwing an undue advantage into
his hands. Several of his pictures were, by permission of their
noble proprietors, available to our purpose ; and, after maturely
balancing the *pros* and *cons* of each, we finally determined on
commencing with Lord Mansfield's picture of Village Politicians. There was yet, however, a difficulty to be got over
regarding this subject, inasmuch as Samuel Reynolds had obtained leave to make a large mezzotinto print from it, and had
even proceeded some way with the plate. A negociation was
therefore entered upon with Reynolds for the purchase of his
right to publish, &c., which ended in Wilkie's payment to

Reynolds of one hundred guineas for his claims, and receiving
from him the plate, which remains unused and unserviceable,
and is likely so to remain. This sum was intended to be charged
on our joint concern, but Wilkie subsequently took it most
liberally upon himself.

Early in this year (1812) he had decided on trying the
success of an exhibition of his works collectively, and for this
object engaged a commodious and well-situated room in Pall
Mall, (No. 87) in which were displayed twenty-nine of his
pictures, ten of which were sketches of larger subjects, then also
in the room, and seven of the remaining nineteen had been
previously seen by the public at the annual exhibition of the
six preceding years at Somerset House. The Wilkie Gallery was by far the most popular exhibition of the day, and
was attended by throngs, while other pictorial attractions were
comparatively deserted by the public. The profits, notwithstanding, were by no means proportionate ; as, in addition to
the necessary expenses of rent, fitting-up, attendants, wages,
advertisements, and posting-bills, a most untoward circumstance
must be added to the debit side of the account — namely, the
seizure of the pictures for rent, due by the person of whom
Wilkie hired the rooms to the original landlord. The distraint
was regularly made, some of the pictures (the Rent Day, Village Holiday, &c.) scheduled at a valuation by the broker, sufficient in his estimation to cover his employer's demand, and a
man in due form placed in possession. The broker, as was his
duty, put a very low price for greater security on the articles
selected, though the sum of ten or twelve pounds for the Rent
Day would seem somewhat ridiculous, from excess of caution.
This vexatious interference was got over, of course, by the one
only method—that of Wilkie paying the debt and costs in the

first instance, and seeking his remedy against the debtor by deducting the future rent accruing for his use of the rooms. He was not so great a loser by this event as was at one time feared he might have been; and something may, I think, be fairly set off if the strong impression made upon Wilkie's mind by the occurrence led, as I believe it did, to the production of one of his pictures of the highest degree of excellence, namely, Distraining for Rent, which was the subject he commenced immediately afterwards.

During the exhibition in Pall Mall, I had cleared off some engagements, and, refusing all others, I was prepared at its close to proceed uninterruptedly with the engraving as soon as the picture was sent to me, and which I received at the latter end of June, 1812. We had previously issued proposals for the print, and had also, at Wilkie's suggestion, inserted in the catalogue of his exhibition a notice on the subject, which, with the reception of names at the room in Pall Mall, procured us some though not a great number of subscribers, paying a deposit at the time. The proofs were to be four guineas each, and the ordinary impressions half that sum. I set to work assiduously, and proceeded without intermission to its termination in October, 1813; having issued the etching, which was favourably received, in the course of the preceding year, and finally completed the engraving in about sixteen months from its commencement, in July, 1812. It was ready for publication on the 1st of January, 1814, and is so dated; but an unusual severity of frost checked the printing for several weeks, so that it did not publicly appear till the beginning of March. Its success at first was not very encouraging; and though I will not say there was much reason for absolute despondency, yet certainly I found none at all for self-congratulation at the result. The printsellers, though compelled by the great popularity of Wilkie to deal in his prints, were nevertheless, naturally as traders, opposed to any enterprize originating out of the pale of their own (as they considered by right) exclusive domain. However, the sale kept creeping on by little and little, though checked perhaps by our having raised the price to non-subscribers, and for more than twenty years never came to a full stop. Two hundred and fifty proofs were printed, besides twenty-four before the insertion of the coat of arms, and the alteration of the etched letters of the title, making together two hundred and seventy four, a number that for some years remained a complete drug on our hands ; so much so, that we sent a large quantity on a venture to America, and never received any tidings of them more. A favourable change has since taken place, and proofs have brought, even at auctions, the extravagant sum of fourteen or fifteen pounds each. A good deal of time was necessarily occupied in superintending the publication, and maintaining a rather extensive correspondence with dealers, English and foreign ; but the interruption in itself was more agreeable than otherwise, and made a cheerful and animated break in the usual secluded and monotonous course of the unsocial life of an engraver. I contrived, however, to fill up intervals of my leisure with an occasional small plate for the booksellers, but was not long before I was earnestly occupied on the engraving from Wilkie's most popular picture of The Rent Day, in Lord Mulgrave's collection, which his lordship very kindly spared for the purpose, during the whole term of two years and a half. It was completed in 1816, but was not published till the beginning of the next year. It not only had the good fortune to meet with great success in itself, but also revived the sale of the drooping Village Politicians. The subscription price was not increased, as in the previous instance, on publication, and this circumstance may probably have contributed to its success. The same number of proofs were taken as of the preceding plate, but there were none entirely finished with the etched letters preserved, as had been done with Village Politicians. A very few (about nine) were printed after the title and dedication had been inserted, while I was waiting for a sketch of Lord Mulgrave's coat of arms, which appears in all the succeeding impressions.

I had pursued my profession very assiduously since my marriage, and the claims of an increasing family were an additional stimulus to exertion, dependent as my children were on my individual labours ; never having found myself able to obtain, though I often attempted, any efficient assistance from others in the art : but my health, hitherto excellent, now seemed giving way. For more than five years preceding the autumn of 1816, I had not slept a night from under my own roof, or been absent an entire day from my engraving-table ; and the sudden and severe domestic calamity I had recently suffered combined with other circumstances to make some relaxation advisable. This led to a little tour in the Netherlands, in the company of my respected friend, Mr. Wilkie, who, joined me at Margate, where my family remained during our trip.

We embarked at Ramsgate for Ostend, in the Eclipse sailing-packet, on the night of Thursday, September 12, 1816, and arrived at Ostend on the following afternoon, proceeding early the next morning by the canal to Bruges, and thence, also by the canal, to Ghent, where we took up our quarters at the Lion d'Or, and finally reached Brussels by the diligence on Sunday evening. The hotels were so crowded with company, chiefly English, that we had some difficulty in finding a lodging for the night, but, after some fruitless applications at different

places, succeeded in obtaining very good accommodation at the
Hôtel de Clarence. In crossing the sea from Ramsgate, though
our passage was by no means rough, Mr. Wilkie was rendered
quite incapable, by sea-sickness, of exercising his pencil in
sketching even the few objects that were within view ; but, on
landing, he quickly recovered, as is usual, from this distressing
complaint ; and, after a night's rest at the Rose, an hotel
kept by an Englishman, we resumed, at a very early hour in
the morning, our journey, or, as it may be called, our voyage,
in the canal-boat, drawn by horses.

Ostend, with its granite quays and noble harbour ; Bruges,
with its venerable antiquity ; and Ghent, with its splendid
buildings and great extent ; cannot be contemplated without
those painful feelings of regret always excited by the spectacle
of departed grandeur. The scanty population and stillness of
the streets form a striking and melancholy contrast to the animated and busy scenes that the cities of England present ;
while the harsh and sullen manners and religious bigotry of the
people are repulsive in the extreme when compared with the
urbane and conciliatory disposition of our lively neighbours, the
French.

The passage by the canal from Bruges to Ghent, monotonous
and tedious as it might be, was not altogether without its *agrémens :* the dinner on board the passage-boat had indeed almost
an European celebrity for excellence of cookery and moderate-
ness of charge. So remarkable was its superiority to ordinary
entertainments of this sort that, although their inherent claims
to remembrance would readily be admitted by those who had
assisted at them, the recent extinction (1839) of the mode of
travelling by canal by the establishment of railroads preserves
them in the memory as a treat that is gone, never to return.

Neither is the mass to be forgotten, which we attended on Sunday morning at the great church of St. Nicholas, unequalled as it was for sublimity of effect by any thing of the kind we had ever witnessed. Ghent also possesses some of the finest *carillons*, (musical chimes) for which the Netherlands generally are remarkable.

Brussels is an extensive and populous city, of which the upper part has a handsome and imposing appearance, resembling on a small scale our Regent's Park buildings, though assuredly not thought little of by the natives, as was evinced by the indignant reply of our astonished cabriolet-driver to a remark I made on the miniature proportions of their beautiful park, situated in the centre of these noble houses : " *Comment, monsieur, petit ? Mais c'est extrèmement grand !* " This quarter of the town has since become colonized, in a manner, by numerous English residents.

On Monday the 16th we started at an early hour, and devoted the day to a visit to the plains of Waterloo, traversing every part of it under the direction of a guide, cutting a branch from the Wellington tree, and making small purchases from the peasantry of the scattered *débris* of the conquered army. The weather was beautiful, and several gay parties of our countrymen and women were busily occupied in exploring the various interesting points of the field of battle, and listening to the anecdotes and stories of the great contest, retailed to them by Lacoste and his comrades ; while the wheat-harvest, unprecedentedly rich, then gathering by the farmers, led to melancholy reflections on its supposed causes, and its contrast of peaceful labour with the horrors of the past year. There was, however, at this time, fifteen months after the event, but little appearance of desolation, except only at the Château of Hougomont, or Gomont. This pretty and retired country residence of a Flemish gentleman had been the scene of the greatest slaughter and destruction, and still shewed many marks of devastation. In a secluded alley in its garden, and marked by a headstone with his name, is the grave of Lieut. John Lucie Blackman, Coldstream Guards, son of Colonel Sir George Blackman, (now Harnage) Bart. Its effect on the spectator in this situation is extremely touching. In another part of the field, the farm of La Haye Sainte, where also the struggle had been tremendous, was now pretty well restored, and the other more distant point, so often named in that great day's history, *La belle Alliance*, had suffered nothing in the contest, and was interesting as having been the place of observation for Napoléon at the commencement, and of Wellington and Blucher's meeting, after the battle. It is a detached road-side common kind of public-house, with which its romantic name is in very little accordance, and was, at the period of our visit, engaged chiefly in the business of selling to strangers the battered reliques of the memorable 18th of June, 1815.

We came back to the little village of Waterloo, about half a mile distant, and dined *Au Quartier Général du Duc de Wellington*, a small inn, so named on its sign-board from having been that of the Duke the night before the battle, and after viewing the memorials of the officers of the guards raised in honour of their slain comrades in Waterloo church, and the adjoining cottage-garden, where Lord Anglesey's leg lies buried, returned to Brussels in the evening, a good deal fatigued, but highly gratified with the day's excursion.

On the 17th we set out in the diligence for Antwerp, passing through Malines, (Mechlin) where we breakfasted and had a cursory sight of the noble cathedral. Antwerp, though sadly fallen from its former greatness, is still a busy and populous city, and contains much to interest a stranger, but our stay was not sufficient to allow of lengthened examination. The appearance of the town was rendered more than usually animated by the annual fair which is held at this season, and attracted great numbers of commercial people. We visited the great church, the citadel, &c.; and at the former were gladdened with the sight of those splendid works of Rubens restored to their legitimate places, which had, fourteen years before, been the objects of my daily contemplation in the Louvre Gallery at Paris. The great altarpiece, the Annunciation of the Virgin, a picture with a circular top, seemed especially to have gained so much by the return to its original situation, as to lead to the belief of its having been painted expressly for it. As to the view from the high tower of the cathedral, so celebrated and so much an object of curiosity with travellers, I can say nothing; as neither Mr. Wilkie nor myself felt disposed to encounter the fatigue of ascending to the summit, for the mere purpose of being able to say we had so done, and of looking over the plain on which Antwerp stands. At the citadel we obtained without difficulty permission from the officer in command to go over the fortification, accompanied by a veteran serjeant of the garrison, but whose explanations, given in French with great earnestness and urbanity, were, from want of knowledge of the subject, at least so far as regards myself, totally thrown away: it is considered one of the strongest fortresses in Europe. A House of Correction within the walls of the citadel excited great interest by the completeness of its system and economy; the numerous prisoners being kept, without any apparent constraint, in the most perfect state of cleanliness, order, and industry.

The time having expired in which I had promised to return,

I took leave most reluctantly of my fellow-traveller, who extended his tour to Holland ; quitted Antwerp in the evening, and crossing the " lazy Scheldt," arrived by the diligence early next morning at Ghent, and, continuing my route in the same way that I came, rejoined my family at Margate.

To resume my professional narrative. A good deal of my time was now necessarily engaged in superintending the printing and keeping the plate in tolerable condition by repeated reparations, as well as by the correspondence and accounts, both abroad and at home, with the dealers ; but though the interruption to my regular pursuits was considerable, I am rather disposed in striking a balance of profit and loss to reckon an occasional compelled change of employment as a beneficial relaxation from the severe study and unsocial occupation of an artist. I also completed at this time some small plates from Smirke's pictures for Cadell's edition of *Don Quixote*, before recommencing the series from Wilkie, of which the next one selected was The Cut Finger, a favourite little picture with the public, which we thought would safely warrant the speculation of a print of half the size and at half the price of the Rent Day. The event scarcely justified our expectations, as its sale has been but indifferent. Blind-man's Buff was the next plate in succession, and obtained a fair measure of success, though very far below that which had attended its predecessors, Village Politicians and The Rent Day. A capital error on our parts regarding this print may be briefly noticed ; namely, the printing of a very large number (five hundred) of proofs ; though that quantity, great as it certainly is, does not reach half the amount that has been taken of impressions under that denomination, from various plates published by the print-sellers. The value of proofs of Village Politicians and The

Rent Day having doubled in the market, led us to believe that we might safely venture to increase in a proportionate degree the number of proofs of Blind-man's Buff, especially as our preliminary subscriptions were numerous and encouraging. The experiment, however, signally failed ; the price continuing the same, or with a small unimportant advance, as at the first publication.

Our next enterprise in this way was The Errand Boy, of the same size and price as The Cut Finger ; the dull sale of which latter was fondly hoped might be re-animated by association with a companion. In this hope we were entirely disappointed, as The Errand Boy failed in his mission altogether ; neither enlivening the torpidity of his predecessor, nor producing any profit in himself. Indeed, when the loss sustained by the bankruptcy of the house of Hurst and Robinson, which took place shortly after its publication, is taken into the account, the print of The Errand Boy may be considered as not having paid its own very moderate expenses.

From the comparative failure of these two prints, we were led to the conclusion that the public were not disposed to favour works of smaller dimensions than those of our earlier publications, and consequently our thoughts were turned to another subject that might justify an expenditure of time equal to the production of an engraving of equal dimensions to those of The Rent Day and the others. The picture of The Reading of a Will, painted for the King of Bavaria, and sent over to Münich, was suggested, and the means of procuring a copy fit for the purpose were maturely considered. Mr. Reinagle was applied to by Mr. Wilkie, but his terms (four hundred guineas, the same sum as was paid for the original) besides travelling expenses, rendered this impracticable. A drawing was afterwards made in black chalk by a native artist at Münich ; but, when it appeared, was found totally inadequate to the purpose.

The difficulty and inconvenience of removing a young family, and the objections to a long residence in a foreign country, particularly for the children, put an end to all notions of my going to Germany for the purpose of engraving from the picture itself, a scheme that was at first suggested. In these circumstances, my attention was directed to the picture of Distraining for Rent, the property of the Directors of the British Gallery, to whom I applied for their permission to make an engraving from it. This was declined ; but the refusal was accompanied with some observations that led to my negotiating with them for the purchase of the picture at the price (six hundred guineas) they had paid for it, and their finally agreeing to receive the amount from me in four instalments of a hundred and fifty guineas each, extended over the term of a year and a half, the first payment to be made on the delivery of the picture. These terms were strictly fulfilled, my friend, Mr. Emmerson, joining with me as collateral security for the faithful performance of my engagement. Mr. Wilkie, with his never-failing sagacity, doubted from the first of the prudence of the undertaking, on the score of its melancholy subject, but waived his objections in compliance with my earnestly expressed wishes. The plate was completed in due time, but the event fully justified Mr. Wilkie's forebodings : the sale was languishing—less successful even than that of Blind-man's Buff; but the picture itself was advantageously disposed of at the price of eight hundred guineas, through the medium of my constant and long-continued friend Emmerson, to Mr. Wells, in whose possession it still (1842) remains, forming one of the most valued and admired ornaments of his very choice collection.

On the completion of the etching of this plate (1824) I made
an excursion of a few weeks to Paris, taking with me as a companion my eldest son, then aged sixteen, the opportunity for
which was afforded by the autumn vacation at Westminster-
school. Of the flattering reception I met with from my
brother-artists, the French engravers, I find it difficult to speak
without unbecoming egotism. I had previously been visited in
London by M. Desnoyers ;[137] and, on the present occasion, I
became also acquainted with most of the other eminent engravers of Paris : Forster,[138] Dupont,[139] Richomme, Leisnier,

[137] Le Baron Desnoyers, officer of the Legion of Honour, member of the
French Institute, and honorary member of the Academies of Milan, Vienna, and Geneva, born in Paris in 1779, the head of the French school
of engraving. Among his finest plates are, a whole-length portrait of Napoléon after Gérard, Francis I. showing to his sister the distich,

" Souvent femme varie :
Bien fol est qui s'y fie—"

which he had been tracing with a diamond on one of the windows at Cham-
bord, from a picture by Richard, and the Vierge au Poisson and Vierge
d'Albe, after Raphael.—M. T. S. R.

[138] Felix Forster, *Chevalier de la Légion d'Honneur*, &c. ; a native of
Switzerland, but long domiciled in Paris. Francis the First receiving
Charles the Fifth, Dido listening to the tale of Æneas, with several beau-
tiful plates after Raphael, by this distinguished artist, are well known in
England.—M. T. S. R.

[139] Henriquel-Dupont, born at Paris in 1797, a pupil of Guérin, and
afterwards of Bervic. Among his most celebrated works are, Gustavus
Vasa, after Hersent; Strafford going to execution, after Paul de la Roche ;
and Christ delivering captives, and consoling the afflicted, after Arry
Sheffer. There are also an exquisite portrait, from a drawing by himself,
of Count Philippe de Ségur, the historian of the Russian Campaign, and a
singularly powerful aquatint of Cromwell gazing on the body of Charles.
—M. T. S. R.

Vallot, &c. ; and have ever since enjoyed a continuance of that
liberal and friendly disposition on their part, that equally
honoured and delighted me at the time. Among the numerous
civilities bestowed, I may perhaps be allowed to mention an
invitation to a sumptuous dinner given at Grignon's, which was
attended by about a dozen artists and amateurs. The whole
affair went off admirably, as is usual in matters of this sort
among the French, and, not to speak of myself, proved especially gratifying to my son, who was kindly pressed into the
party by our liberal, warm-hearted friend, Forster. The reception generally of English artists in Paris is flattering in
the extreme, and still the more generous on the part of the
French, as I fear we are sadly deficient in reciprocity of conduct. Without adverting to others, I do not hesitate to avow
in respect to myself the deepest acknowledgments. In the *salon*
(exhibition) of 1814, the engraving of Village Politicians was
placed by one of our Parisian agents. The print was then
newly published, and excited some notice, as also, perhaps fortunately, a good deal of sharp criticism, shewing at least that
it was not considered beneath observation. For this a gold
medal was awarded by the committee of adjudication, and
which I duly received through the medium of Mr. C. Mac-
kenzie, one of the secretaries of our embassy. It has, on one
side, a head of the king, beautifully executed by the celebrated
Andrieu, with the inscription—Louis XVIII. Roi de France et
de Navarre ; on the reverse—Exposition au Salon de 1814.
Mr. Raimbach, de Londres, Graveur.

Small as the honour may be, I felt it as a great distinction,
in the absence of all academical reward or encouragement in my
own country ; and how much was this feeling increased when
afterwards, in 1835, I was elected a corresponding Member of

the Institute of France! To shew that being thus noticed was no slight compliment, there needs but a glance at the names of the distinguished men of every country in Europe, which form the annually published list of this unequalled assemblage of art, science, and philosophy.[140] Of English artists admitted into this association, are Wilkie, Cockerell, and Donaldson ; while, on the other hand, not even a single instance can be quoted in which our Royal Academicians have ever manifested an honorary recognition of foreign contemporary talent. Invidious contrast! not less mortifying than discreditable, that our academy annals should not only never have been graced by the names of such men as Canova, Thorwaldsen, Gérard, and Morghen, but that the courtesy of an advantageous place in our exhibition has been almost invariably refused to the works of foreign artists, and, in many instances, their pictures of, at least, average merit rejected altogether : a system of mean and narrow exclusiveness, that would well

[140] The following is an extract of a letter from Sir David Wilkie to Abraham Raimbach, Esq., on the occasion of their being elected corresponding members of the Academy of Fine Arts in the French Institute.
                                                              M. T. S. R.

                                                    "Kensington, Dec. 13th, 1835.
    "Your very obliging letter conveyed to me the first notice of what has since appeared in most of the papers—the strangers that have been elected corresponding members of the Institute of France ; among whom you may be assured I was exceedingly gratified to find that your own and my name were included. This is a distinction to which my art could in no case have arrived, confined from its nature to one place, were it not that it has been fortunately combined with yours, the excellence and beauty of which are wafted forth on a thousand wings, and speak simultaneously to all countries and in all languages."

warrant the application of the line of the French satirist—
"*Nul n'aura de l'esprit, hors nous et nos amis.*"—Boileau.
Many such occurrences might be quoted, but the following, one
of the most recent, will sufficiently illustrate this dominant and
invidious conduct.

In the first year's exhibition in their new apartments in
Trafalgar Square (1837), a picture of cabinet size was presented
for admission by M. Gudin, the French marine-painter, and
was at first refused, but, on the indignant remonstrance of
more than one academician on the discredit which such a proceeding towards an eminent foreigner would reflect on their
society, it was afterwards admitted, *but only on condition that
one of the remonstrators* (Mr. W. Daniell) should withdraw one
of his own pictures already received, of similar dimensions.
The condition was at once acceded to by Mr. W. Daniell, and
rigidly enforced by the academy, who justified this harsh proceeding on the plea of want of sufficient space in their rooms for
works of superior claims. It required, however, but little
critical knowledge to perceive at a glance over the exhibition,
that Gudin's *La Détresse*, as his picture was named, possessed
more interest in its subject, a shipwreck, and displayed more
talent in its execution, than scores of the gay works which surrounded it. During my stay in Paris, in 1824, one of the
chief attractions was the *Salon*, as the collection of works of
living artists is called ; and it was highly gratifying to observe
the sensation produced by Sir Thomas Lawrence's pictures,
two of which (portraits of the Duc de Richelieu and of Mrs.
Harford) he had sent for exhibition.

The next year (1825) my whole family, escorted by my
eldest son, went on a visit to my wife's mother, who resided in
Paris, and remained there near two months, I joining the party

during the last three weeks of the time, my son being obliged
to return to his studies at Westminster. This expedition was
a somewhat memorable occurrence in my secluded and little-
eventful course, more especially as there were two children of
the party, of the respective ages of two and five years. The
excursion afforded me, as usual, much gratification in renewing
my acquaintance with the French artists, and increasing our
friendly intercourse. Several of our most distinguished painters
were at this period in Paris—Sir Thomas Lawrence, Mr.
Wilkie, Mr. Alfred Chalon, &c., &c. Sir Thomas Lawrence
was engaged on the portraits of the King (Charles X.) and
the Duchess of Berri, and received from his Majesty the
ribbon of the Legion of Honour. Sir Thomas, with great kindness, at my request, sent to my hotel his beautiful picture of
Mr. Calmady's children (since admirably engraved by Doo),
for the purpose of enabling me to shew it to my French
friends.[141] I had previously been introduced to Sir Thomas
Lawrence by Mr. Wilkie in London, and had also met him at
Mr. Wilkie's lodgings in Paris, previous to the departure of
the latter for a tour in Switzerland and Italy, in hopes of re-

[141] Sir Thomas Lawrence's note, in which he accedes to my father's
request, is as follows.—M. T. S. R.

"Hôtel de Londres, Place Vendôme, Sept. 30th.

"Dear Sir,

"I am much honoured by your friends' desire to see the picture you
mention, and feel additional pleasure in believing that it is owing to your
partial report of it. At present it is not in my possession, but I shall have
it about Wednesday or Thursday next, a period not, I hope, too late for its
being shewn to them by you. I will either send it to you, or request the
favour of a visit from you with your friends, one of whom may, in fair reci-

establishing his shattered health, which had been declining greatly since the rude shock it had received by the death of his mother.

Among the most gratifying attentions I received was an invitation to dinner by the Baron Gérard, where the guests, about eight in number, included Sir Thomas Lawrence, M. Raoul-Rochette, the antiquary, and M. Meyerbeer, the musical composer, and forming a very choice specimen of the elegance, politeness, and freedom from ceremonial of a high-class French entertainment. In the evening there was a numerous assemblage of persons, more than a hundred, many of them distinguished characters, of whom M. Pozzo di Borgo, the Russian Ambassador, seemed, however, to be considered the most important personage. All the leading opera-singers, Zuchelli, Bordogni, Pellegrini, and Signora Mombelli, accompanied on the pianoforte by the celebrated Paër, a fine player as well as composer, contributed their exquisite talents (I suppose *not* gratuitously) in forming a most delicious musical treat. Ices and refreshments of various kinds were served in profusion, and a superb billiard-table in an adjoining apartment, brilliantly lighted up, diversified the amusements of the *soirée*, and had many votaries, chiefly among the Italians of the party, some of whom played remarkably well. Zuchelli was introduced by Pellegrini, the painter, to Sir Thomas Lawrence, as having been in Rome at the same time with Sir Thomas, in

procity, look on my works with some indulgence, in return for the high admiration which I have often felt of his distinguished talents.

"Pray have the goodness to give me some days' notice of your departure, and in the mean time believe me to remain,

"Dear Sir,

"Your obliged and faithful servant,

"THOMAS LAWRENCE."

1818, and apologised for his broken English, though it was his native language, he having been born, I believe, in Ireland, of foreign parents.

This *fête*, given by Baron Gérard, as I was made to understand, in honour of Sir Thomas Lawrence, was an appropriate and becoming compliment from the chief of the arts in one country to the corresponding rank in another. It took place at the Baron's summer residence at Auteuil, about three miles from Paris, a handsome house, tastefully fitted up, formerly belonging to Decrès, Bonaparte's Minister of Marine. The principal rooms were spacious and well proportioned, and all on the ground-floor; one of them was ornamented, by direction of the Minister, with fresco paintings of sea-ports, shipping, &c., and communicated with the extensive garden by a balconied terrace outside, to which the company were invited in the course of the evening to view the comet, which happened, from the great clearness of the atmosphere, to be then visible in uncommon splendour (October, 1825). Soon after eleven o'clock the party began to break up; and, as our coachman drove us through the courtyard and places adjoining, we had some difficulty in threading the maze of crowded carriages of all descriptions that were in waiting.

The Baron Gérard, the pupil and successor of David as the head of that school of art which the latter had founded, was an Italian by birth, and was thought by some persons to combine with his acknowledged talents as an artist and the manners and address of a gentleman something of the Machiavelian policy of his country. His works are well known, and, like those of others of the same school, such as Gros, Girodet, and Guérin, display many admirable qualities, and great power of execution. It may, however, be doubted whether any of them are destined to take a permanent place in the ranks of those whose works have been tested by the rigid and uninfluenced ordeal of revolving years, and whose names are familiar to us as "household words." M. Gérard was accustomed to hold a meeting or *conversazione* once a week at his house in Paris, which was continued many years, and was resorted to by artists, men of letters, actors, musicians, &c.; while Madame Gérard, receiving her lady-friends at the same time, it formed altogether a most agreeable re-union; as can be testified by many English artists, towards whom the Baron was generally disposed to shew a highly flattering degree of civility and attention.

In person M. Gérard was rather below the middle stature, with a cast of features resembling the physiognomy of the late John Kemble; Sir Thomas Lawrence remarking to me that the Baron reminded him strongly of his lamented friend. Sir Thomas painted the Baron's portrait while in Paris, and presented it to Madame Gérard. The annual distribution of medals in the class of the fine arts in the Institute occurring during my stay in Paris, I had the good fortune to receive from one of the members, M. Desnoyers, a ticket, admitting me to the body of the hall where this interesting ceremony took place. M. Gros presided on the occasion, and the scene was graced by a brilliant show of ladies in addition to the crowd of gentlemen. The proceedings displayed some peculiarities, highly characteristic and exciting to the curiosity of the English part of the assemblage. A few words from the President opened the sitting, and was followed by a statement read by M. Garnier, relative to the progress of the class, and commendatory of the merits of the concurrents, more especially those of the successful candidates. The medals were then delivered by the President to the fortunate competitors, accompanied with a brief

complimentary address to each, as they respectively made way
to the rostrum on their names being called in succession. Immediately afterwards each medalist rushed to his instructor
(usually a member of the Institute), seated in the first circle
of the amphitheatre, and, with repeated and vehement kisses
on both sides of the face, thus gave vent to his grateful and delighted feelings, which next overflowed in the same way to his
nearest relations then present. The presentation of each
medal was attended with applause, more or less enthusiastic
and vociferous, particularly from the numerous students in the
gallery, according to the degree in which the award of the
judges coincided with the opinion of the auditory. There was,
however, one, and *only* one exception to this unison of sentiment throughout. This happened in an instance where the
fairest claim was said to have been superseded by undue
influence ; and a burst of indignant clamour ensued on announcing the name, that made the very walls of the *Quatre-
Nations* to vibrate. The perpetual Secretary of the class of fine
arts, M. Quatremère de Quincy, now read a long dissertation,
which, being followed by some well-executed prize pieces of
music, both vocal and instrumental, by an excellent orchestra
of performers, very pleasantly terminated the solemnities of
the day.

Many of the members of the Institute and some of the
ministers were present. Among the artists I perceived Gros,
Garnier, Vernet, and Ingres. Gérard was absent. The only
drawback, to my entire satisfaction, was in observing our distinguished countryman, Lawrence, enter the hall and proceed
to one of the seats open to the public, without introduction or
any kind of ceremony ; and after remaining to the end utterly
unnoticed, was finally suffered to quit the Hall without the

smallest mark of respect or recognition whatever. As I felt somewhat indignant at this apparent neglect of our celebrated artist, I could not refrain from expressing my surprise to a French friend at this seeming want of courtesy, when he assured me that the powers of Lawrence, as a portrait-painter, were admitted to a certain degree, but that his acquirements as an artist generally were estimated rather cheaply by the painters of the Institute, who considered themselves as holding in quality of historical painters a much higher grade in the profession. Sir Thomas wore the red ribbon of the Legion of Honour. I had occasion to observe afterwards that the kind of diplomatic state and style of procedure he had very properly adopted, as commissioned by one monarch to another, was made a subject of ridicule by the French, who, although the kingly government has been restored, have certainly not regained their ancient loyalty and veneration for the throne.

At the latter end of October I brought my family back to London, without any mishap, and have not since, to my great regret, found it convenient to visit *la belle France*. On my return to England, after this excursion, so replete as it had been with interest and enjoyment, it required no small effort on my part to take up again the monotonous and solitary duties of my profession ; but much may be done by dogged resolution in a case of necessity. Thus, having resumed my labours on the plate of Distraining for Rent, I proceeded without further interruption to its completion. Of all my larger plates from Wilkie, this has been the least successful ; still it did not founder so completely as the little Errand Boy. It is only doing justice to the soundness of Wilkie's judgment to state that he considered the subject so objectionable (having indeed proved it by the difficulty he experienced in disposing of the picture) that he strongly advised me to relinquish the speculation ; but I was too enthusiastic in my admiration of the picture to be deterred by the distressful nature of the story so vividly told in it.   The extreme popularity too of the painter, though always great, had begun to diminish, and the public favour, after flowing near twenty years in one direction, required, as usual, the excitement of novelty or a change of some sort.   But though Distraining for Rent was comparatively unsuccessful, it was by no means an absolute failure, as before observed.   There were gradations in the fortune of the respective plates, of which that of the Errand Boy may be set down at zero, and those of The Cut Finger, Distraining for Rent, Blind-man's Buff, Village Politicians, and The Rent Day at different degrees of elevation in the scale of success.   The sale of The Rent Day has reached the number of between four and five thousand impressions, and still (1842) five-and-twenty years after its first publication, continues in a small way ; the same may be said of Village Politicians and of Blind-man's Buff, in a yet minor degree.   Very considerable and constant reparations were of course rendered necessary by the wear and tear of the plates in the process of printing, amounting in some cases to as much time probably, in their execution, as might have sufficed for a re-engraving of the plate.

Mr. Wilkie was not of robust constitution ; but with great temperance, careful management, and judicious relaxation from the arduous practice of his art, his general state of health was such as to enable him to pursue his profession without any material interruption.   In the year 1820, he made a fortnight's excursion to Norfolk, in which I had the honour of accompanying him, on an invitation to our old and very kind friend, the Reverend Mr. Adams, the rector of Edingthorpe, and more than once he had visited his relations and friends in Scotland. During his absence from home on one of these latter, he had the misfortune to lose his kind-hearted, excellent mother, who had been long declining, and shortly after his own health showed symptoms of seriously giving way. The usual consultations of surgeons and physicians led to a recommendation of a decided change of scene, and the abstaining for a time from all professional occupation.

Mr. Wilkie, acting on this advice, made a lengthened tour of more than two years in France, Switzerland, Italy, and Spain, and returned to England in 1828, with health happily re-established. He brought with him the series of pictures he had executed in Spain, now in the royal collection, having been purchased by George IV. Wilkie resumed his system of having engravings made from his works, and having obtained the loan of the picture of Chelsea Pensioners reading the Gazette of Waterloo from the Duke of Wellington, and that of The Parish Beadle from Mr. Ridley Colborne (now Lord Colborne), proceeded to put them in hand forthwith. The Chelsea Pensioners, engraved on a large scale, would of course be a long and laborious undertaking, and after maturely considering the various circumstances of the necessity of uniting in the enterprise with the printsellers Mess. Moon, Boys, and Graves, I was induced to decline the offer, preferring to accept from the same firm the commission of engraving The Parish Beadle, at the price of sixteen hundred guineas. Neither of these subjects proved successful as speculations, I believe, notwithstanding the advantageous means possessed by the publishers of extensive circulation, or, according to the mercantile phrase, of "forcing a sale," both at home and abroad. Before the completion of my plate, I had some reason to fear that the firm,

now fallen into embarrassments, together with the secession
of the principal partner, Moon, might prevent the fulfilment of
their engagement to me; but, after a good deal of delay, and by
their having fortunately found a moneyed partner in Mr.Richard
Hodgson, I was honourably paid the whole amount of the sum
agreed on for my engraving.

The delicate health of my son David requiring a permanent
change of air, led in autumn, 1831, to my fixing our family
residence, after sufficient proof of its beneficial effect in the
vicinity of Greenwich, close to the beautiful Park of that well-
known town.   With some of the advantages of a country retreat, this place has pre-eminently many of the inconveniences
of a retirement from London, more especially when that retirement is only to a short distance from the metropolis.   The
delicious purity and sweetness of the air of Greenwich Park,
Blackheath, and the neighbouring villages, forms a principal
and certainly a very important item in the list of benefits, to
which may be added its comparative quietude and stillness,
without losing a facility, cheapness, and rapidity of communication with the great centre of the civilized world, that ren-
ders it almost identical with an actual residence in the suburbs.
On the other hand, among its drawbacks may be numbered
the serious one of greater expensiveness of living—all articles
of housekeeping being invariably at a higher price—from ten
to twenty per cent—than in London, or than in the country,
properly so called.   The absurd and ridiculous excess to which
in private life the middle classes of England carry their notions
of etiquette, in regard to rank, station, and fortune, is displayed
to a most amusing degree by the exclusives of Greenwich, where
the *élite* of the population consists of tradesmen out of business,
clerks in public offices, some members of the Stock Exchange,

of Lloyd's, of Mark Lane, together with the usual indigenous
village muster, of law, physic, and divinity, concentrating, in a
narrow space, all the less amiable characteristics of *society*, as
it is called — vain, frivolous, intolerant, calumnious, over-
bearing !

> " 'Tis pleasant, through the loophole of retreat,
> To peep at such a world ; to see the stir
> Of the great Babel, and not feel the crowd "—

These remarks, of a mere looker-on, though rather extrane-
ous, may be excused as the spontaneous result of an experience of more than ten years residence (1842).

After the completion of the engraving of the Parish Beadle,
and having no immediate expectation of another professional
engagement, I set doggedly to work in repairing the plates of
Village Politicians, The Rent Day, and Blind-man's Buff,
which had printed, particularly the two former, a large number of impressions, and were now running to almost cure-
less ruin. This necessarily occupied a considerable time, and
in no very agreeable way ; but it was time and labour well-be
stowed, inasmuch as the popularity of the subjects was not
exhausted, and the sale of the prints, though small, did not
cease altogether ; while the plates, being brought to a sound
and serviceable state, were rendered capable of producing a
great many more impressions of at least a decent appearance ;
to restore them to their pristine bloom and vigour was quite
out of the question.

In the year 1834, Mr. Wilkie painted for Sir William
Knighton the picture of the Spanish Mother, and a proposition
was made to me and accepted, that I should execute an engraving from it. Sir William was a great favourite with

George IV., and held an office in the household. His intimacy
with Wilkie arose from the attendance of the latter occasionally at the palace in obedience to the royal command, and
which ultimately led to the placing the present baronet, Sir
W. Wellesley Knighton, as a pupil with Wilkie, though of
course not with any view of his following it up by professional
practice. On the completion of the plate, a negotiation was
entered into for the purchase of it by Moon, the printseller,
and also by Hodgson and Graves, which finally terminated in
the disposal of it to the former, at the price of seven hundred
and fifty guineas, which he honourably paid before its publication, in 1836. Notwithstanding some degree of novelty in the
subject, as regards the usual class of Wilkie's pictures selected
for engraving, and the exercise of the various means by which
the dealers are thought to be able to promote a sale of their
own publications, The Spanish Mother did not meet with
the favourable reception as a print that was expected by the
adventurous speculator. Probably the inadequacy of my execution was a main cause of its ill-success ; but however that
might be, (and I certainly do not mean, nor would it become
me to dispute it,) I think there were other causes in action
about this time that may have contributed to this comparative
failure. For the long term of more than twenty years the
prints from Wilkie's pictures had enjoyed an almost unprecedented popularity ; and it can scarcely be held as a matter of
reproach to the public if, after so long a period of favour in one
direction, the desire of some sort of change of object should be
entertained. The great talents of Edwin Landseer had been
already well appreciated, when his picture of the Monks of
Bolton Abbey appeared, and placed his reputation on a still
higher elevation. Seconded by Cousins's admirable mezzo-

tinto from it, there followed a rush in the track thus so auspiciously commenced, and the new lights (as in Aladdin's lamp) were preferred to the old. However this state of matters may continue for a time, the sterling qualities of Wilkie are sure, in the long run, to establish themselves in permanent supremacy in his department of art.

Another and very important cause for the change that had come over the fortunes of the good old legitimate art of line-engraving should not pass unnoticed; namely, the enormous sums now for the first time exacted by the painters under the claim of copyright; a claim, however founded, hitherto left in abeyance at least, if not considered altogether abandoned. The printsellers, in yielding to these claims, sought to indemnify themselves by adopting a more expeditious and lower-priced mode of engraving (mezzotinto), and which, being also executed on steel, enabled them by printing much longer numbers than copper-plates will produce to obtain their usual regular profits. As far as I am aware, this claim of copyright in pictures has only been put forward recently, and is not unlikely to become a *quæstio vexata* between the painters and their patrons, whenever one of the latter shall feel disposed to stand upon his hitherto unquestioned power in these matters of doing what he likes with his own. A noble lord, a great collector of the modern as well as of the old masters, was desirous of befriending a young engraver of talent by allowing him to make an engraving from a picture in his gallery; when the painter, hearing of the circumstance, interfered and prevented the fulfilment of his lordship's benevolent intention, the patron being unwilling to enter into a contest on the subject. How far the painter's claim may be ultimately established is not to be predicted; but in my opinion it will scarcely survive the

first collision it might have to encounter in a court of law. Be
that as it may, the policy of the painter's proceedings may
well admit of a doubt. The patronage of the fine arts is a plant
of too sensitive a nature to bear the rude touch of legal discussion, and many gentlemen well inclined to foster and
encourage genius, would perhaps rather forego their inclination
than indulge it, coupled with the chance of a lawsuit, if resolved to maintain the ordinary privileges identified with property. At all events, the artist should distinctly make known
to the purchaser the conditions with which his picture is encumbered before the bargain is completed, to the end that the
unsuspecting Mæcenas may not have just reason to complain of
uncandid, if not dishonourable dealing, when, after years of possession, the claim of copyright is put forward. Another form
in which this claim has been urged is, that the proprietor of
the picture, having given up the copyright to the painter, thereby
precludes himself from the power of bestowing the privilege to
any other person at a future time. Although perhaps less pre-
sumptuous than the first mode, this has been in two or three
instances somewhat contemptuously resisted.

I continued to occupy myself with occasionally repairing
one or other of my old plates ; when, after many unavailing
suggestions had been made to the printsellers of pictures for
engraving, the publisher, Moon, was induced to apply to me on
the subject of making a print of rather a large size from that
noble work the Columbus, in the collection of Mr. Holford.
With much consultation with Wilkie, and ample consideration
of all circumstances, I gave in my estimate, which we both
agreed was on a very moderate scale, and which indeed could
not be objected to—nor was it on that score, when the time and
labour required to execute a highly-finished line-engraving

were taken into the account. In the terms proposed, I had
shewn myself willing to make a large sacrifice in regard to price,
from the desire to continue the series of prints, and my great
admiration of the picture. Notwithstanding these efforts, it
was found impossible to bring the trader to our way of thinking ;
and the negotiation finally terminated in his declaration of opinion that in the state of discouragement into which engraving
had fallen of late years, he thought it would be imprudent to
risk the adventure. He therefore felt compelled, as a commercial
man, to decline that which, as a sincere lover of art, he was
most anxious to promote: Columbus ultimately appeared as a
mezzotinto print. After this transaction with Moon, a somewhat similar one took place with Hodgson, of Pall Mall, who
proposed to me the engraving a small picture by Raphael, in
the collection of Samuel Rogers, the poet. The size, price,
&c., were all arranged and were agreed on, when the quarrel
arose between Hodgson and his partner Graves, which led to
the retirement of the former, and the abandonment, in consequence, of the engagement with me.

   Referring to some observations on the painter's claim of copyright in a preceding page, it would appear by the following
extract from *Galignani's Messenger* of the latter end of May
1842, that a claim of the same kind had been raised by the
French painters, a branch of which claim had been litigated for
some years, and was now finally adjudicated by the Supreme
Court, that the sale of a picture by the artist, unless accompanied with conditions at the time, conveyed with it also the
right to engrave and publish a print from it, &c. Extract.
" Copyright of Pictures.—The Court of Cassation has decided
the question, whether the sale of a painting by the artist,
without any condition or reserve, conveyed to the purchaser

the exclusive right of taking and publishing an engraving of it ?
The question arose out of the picture of the Battle of the Py-
ramids, painted by Baron Gros in 1809, by order of the Imperial Government, but not delivered before the Restoration,
during which it was carefully concealed by General Bertrand.
Baron Gros had, however, granted permission to M. Vallot to
make an engraving from it. The painting had latterly been
purchased by the Civil List for the Museum at Versailles, and
M. Gavard included it in his series of engravings taken from
those galleries. On its appearance, actions for piracy were commenced against M. Gavard, by the widow of Baron Gros and
M. Vallot. These have taken the round of the different courts
with varying decisions, and at length were brought on an appeal before the Supreme Court, which has decided that the
entire property of the picture passes with it on a sale, and the
consequent right to make and publish engravings from it,
unless there be in the contract or bill of sale an express reserve or stipulation to the contrary. The appeal has therefore
been dismissed with costs."

In the year 1841 I was applied to by M. Ambron, agent
and co-proprietor of an Italian publication, of which an elaborate prospectus had been issued, announcing a series of engravings from the celebrated pictures in the great Florence
Gallery, to be executed by the various European engravers.
After several interviews and pre-arrangements made with M.
Ambron, my name was inserted with those of others, French
and English, and I made a choice of two or three in the list of
subjects, from which one was to be selected for my engraving.
Of this enterprise, also, I heard no more. In regard to this
class of publications, it is difficult to account for the constant
renewal of schemes of serial or continuous works in art, not-

withstanding the almost invariable ill-success that has hitherto attended them. It forms a striking instance of the triumph of hope over disappointment. To name a few only that are within my own recollection : the first and greatest, that of the French Museum by Robillard and Laurent, though well sustained by abundant capital, the highest professional talent, and very skilful direction, during a long course of varying fortunes, finally terminated in a heavy loss. In England, the respective works published by Forster and by Tomkins, of engravings from pictures by the old masters in the collections of the English nobility and gentry ; the prints by the associated engravers of some of the paintings in the National Gallery ; the publication of the Messrs. Finden, of engravings from the works of modern English masters, not to mention the countless numbers of annuals, which at the outset were greatly encouraged, have all, after different terms of existence more or less short, sunk into oblivion.

To the introduction of steel-engraving, by multiplying almost indefinitely the number of impressions each plate would produce, may in a great degree be attributed the decline and debasement of the art, exercised on a small scale. The embellishments of books are no longer what they have been, and the recent discovery and application of the electrotype bids fair to effect similar results as regards works of a large size. This most ingenious process has the power of reproducing, and at a comparatively small expense, any number of fac-similes of the original plate, so perfect as not to be distinguishable from it, whereby an indefinite amount of prints, all equally good, may be taken from them, consequently, greatly lessening the value of the aggregate, and destroying, at the same time, root and branch, the long established system of proofs and early impressions,

which contributed so much to the advantage and respectability
of the profession, by holding out inducements to connoisseurs
and lovers of rarity, to form collections of choice exemplars.
The electrotype has not yet been brought into full activity, nor
indeed can it ever be unless by the discovery of some means of
effecting a prodigious increase and multiplication of print-
buyers, a task of great difficulty, if we may form our judgment
upon the very slow progress that has hitherto been made in the
dissemination and cultivation of a taste for the fine arts among
the bulk of the population in this country.   It is certain that
on the continent—in France, in Holland, in Italy, in Germany—
the masses of the people shew more feeling for these matters ;
and the feeling is more widely diffused than is found in the
same classes in England, notwithstanding our establishments of
the Royal Academy, and the Society for the Encouragement of
Art, have now existed full three quarters of a century.   It
would almost seem as if the state of the fine arts (stationary, if
not retrograde) in this country, is considered as a national reproach, seeing the extraordinary efforts making everywhere in
the formation of societies, and schemes of various kinds for
their encouragement and improvement.   Most of the great
towns and some of the smaller have their Art-Union ; and the
prodigious success of that in London would augur well for its
object, were it not shrewdly suspected that a very large proportion of its eleven thousand members (1842) are stimulated
rather by the lottery which forms the basis of its plan than by
a worthier and more legitimate motive.   And even should
Art-Unions become as numerous in the land as are Dispen-
saries for the Poor, it may still be doubted whether this
forcing system is best adapted to produce the results that
are looked forward to.   A more dignified effort for the same

object is, that making by the government in their appointment of the committee of noblemen and gentlemen, with Prince Albert at the head, to consider how far the embellishment of the new houses of parliament may be made auxiliary to the progress and cultivation of the higher walks of art. This committee, constituted as it is, will certainly feel bound to do something that shall look, at least, like encouragement. They have begun with great spirit, and the munificent premiums already announced leave nothing to be desired on the score of liberality of offer ; it remains to be seen how far it will be responded to by a proportionate display of zeal and talent on the part of the painters, who must now cease their long-continued complaint of the want of government patronage for the higher branches of art.

The lamented death of my respected friend, Sir David Wilkie, ultimately led to the disposal of the plates, our joint property, at the sale by auction of his various works, in the spring of 1842. By his last will, made in 1825, he desired that every thing he died possessed of should be sold for the benefit of his heirs ; and although Mr. Thomas Wilkie and Miss Wilkie, and the sole surviving executor, Sir James M'Grigor, were desirous of adopting any arrangement I might suggest, had I been inclined to retain the sole property of the plates, I determined, after mature deliberation, to avail myself of the opportunity, as the most favourable that could occur for realizing whatever value they had as a marketable commodity. Had any of my family been qualified with the knowledge of engraving and printselling, necessary to enable them to turn this species of property to fair account, I should, perhaps, have decided otherwise ; but none of my children having adopted my own profession, (certainly I never wished that they should, being always too strongly im-

L

pressed with the preponderance of its disadvantages to encourage any such views) it would, in all probability, have remained either sterile and utterly unproductive in my family, or to be finally parted with in less promising circumstances. The six plates and the stock of prints were sold at Christie and Manson's, on the 3rd of May, 1842, as part of the great Wilkie sale, and produced nine hundred and seventy pounds, four shillings ; one lot (Distraining for Rent) having been knocked down to me for seventy-three pounds ten shillings, being within the amount previously arranged with the auctioneers, as a protection price.

The following are the sums for which they sold, and the names of the respective purchasers. I have been given to understand by those who are well experienced in such matters, that these prices are unprecedently good, as compared with similar property brought to the hammer.

	£.	s.	d.	
Village Politicians . . .	367	10	0	Graves and Co.
Rent Day	210	0	0	Gibbs.
Blind-man's Buff	204	15	0	Gibbs.
Distraining for Rent . .	73	10	0	Raimbach.
Cut Finger	64	1	0	Gibbs.
Errand Boy	50	8	0	Shirley.

Here ends the manuscript. But little remains for me to add. On my return home, in the autumn of 1842, after an absence of five years in India and China, I was not less surprised than shocked at the alteration which had taken place in my father's appearance. I felt that he was approaching his end, and, after

I joined the guard-ship at Plymouth, to which I had been appointed, expected every day to hear of his serious illness.

On the ninth of November I received a letter, from which the following is an extract: " You will be surprised to learn that I have been applied to by the Irish Art-Union Society, to engrave for them a large plate, on very handsome, indeed liberal terms (about fifteen hundred guineas). Perhaps you will be more surprised that I have refused it; but I did not at all like the subject, (the fisherman's drowned child) and was not satisfied with the picture, besides my objections to working against time, &c. I have had three interviews with Mr. Blacker, the honorary secretary, a perfect gentleman, with which I had every reason to feel gratified." This was his last transaction connected with art.

He died on the seventeenth of January, 1843, after a very short illness, from water on the chest, within a month of the completion of his sixty-seventh year. It would be impertinent in me to tell of the grief felt by his family for the loss of one so dear; but those who knew him best will best appreciate the affectionate regret with which the memory of so good a man must ever be cherished by those for whom he did so much and made such sacrifices.

In person my father was short and stoutly built. In his youth, as I have been told by his early friends, he was somewhat remarkable for his activity and skill in the manly exercises proper to his age. But in the decline of life, the close confinement of his laborious and sedentary occupation had encouraged a constitutional tendency to corpulency. His countenance, though not regularly handsome, was admirably adapted for the expression of every passing shade of feeling or thought, ever varying, and always full of meaning. There are three good portraits of him in existence : one by Sir David Wilkie, painted in 1818, an admirable little picture, as well as an excellent likeness at that time ; another, of sixteen or seventeen years later date, by M. Duval le Camus, and a medallion by M. Gatteaux, both of them striking resemblances.

It is unnecessary for me to speak of his reputation as an artist, sufficiently well established among those who take any interest in engravers and their productions.   But as, among the honorary distinctions he received from foreign Academies, that conferred by the French Institute was most peculiarly gratifying to him, and as he felt the admiration of his works in France to be a just source of pride and satisfaction, I shall venture to conclude my short notice with a passage from the pen of a distinguished French critic on art, M. Feuillet de Conches.

" Nul artiste n'est plus connu que l'est M. Raimbach, par ses estampes d'après Wilkie, les Politiques de Village, le Jour de Loyer, le Colin Maillard, &c., ses planches pour les Mille et une Nuits, pour Gil Blas, pour Don Quixote, et tant d'autres œuvres admirables, qui ont fait de lui le restaurateur de l'art de la gravure en Angleterre, et qui, avec les œuvres de nos maîtres, n'ont pas peu contribué en France à imprimer une meilleure direction à cette branche importante des arts du dessin.   Quand, aux premiers temps de la restauration, la gravure Anglaise fit son entrée triomphante en France, les productions sérieuses et fortes de M. Raimbach furent distinguées entre toutes et devinrent classiques dans nos ateliers ; et, depuis la revolution de Juillet, l'Institut, qui n'avait jamais admis de correspondant étranger dans la classe de gravure, a voulu faire exception pour lui seul."

M. T. S. R.

MEMOIR

OF

SIR DAVID WILKIE.

MEMOIR

OF

SIR DAVID WILKIE.

David Wilkie is the third son of the Reverend David Wilkie, a clergyman of the Scottish Church, and was born at his father's manse, at Cults, in Fifeshire, on the 19th of November, 1785. David showed at an early age the very common propensity of children to imitate in drawing objects that engage their juvenile fancy, and was encouraged in his youthful efforts by the approbation and advice of his eldest brother, who had himself evinced some indications of a similar taste and disposition. When about fifteen years old, David was sent to Edinburgh for the purpose of studying in the Academy of Design, established there by Mr. Graham, an artist, who had practised some time in London with but little success. In this school Wilkie diligently pursued his course, under the superintendence, and with the advice of Graham, with the view of making painting his profession, and in 1805 came " to seek his fortune" in the great metropolis, and happily and worthily found it. He brought with him to the modern Babylon small store of worldly goods (narrowed by his venerable parent's limited means), but was rich in the possession of genius, industry, and perseverance ;

and, above all, in prudence, integrity, and good principles. He found a friendly reception by the Stodarts, of Golden Square, distant relations of his family, and derived some facilities from letters he brought with him ; among them was one to Caleb Whitefoord [1], the presentation of which originated some years afterwards the picture of The Letter of Introduction. His first residence in London was at Aldgate, but this quarter of the town was so totally out of the world of art, that he very soon quitted it for the more genial atmosphere of Norton Street, Fitzroy Square, as more suited to his views, and being in the neighbourhood of artists of all descriptions.

While lodging there, in a very humble back parlour, he prepared two pictures, Village Politicians and The Sunday Morning; diligently attending the drawing at the Royal Academy in the evenings, and making the acquaintance of some of the members of that institution, as well as of many of the students of its schools : among the former, Flaxman, Northcote, and Fuseli ; and of the latter, Mulready [2], Haydon,

---

[1] "'The best-humour'd man with the worst-humour'd muse."—Goldsmith's *Retaliation*.

[2] William Mulready was born in Ireland, but has passed his life from a very early age in this country. His pictures are not numerous, but when their excellence is considered, and it is at the same time recollected that his time has been mainly occupied in teaching drawing for a subsistence, it may well raise a doubt as to the existence of a national taste for art in England.

Benjamin Robert Haydon, son of a bookseller at Plymouth, is one of those geniuses whose irregular practice dooms them to " eat mutton cold, and cut blocks with a razor." Indignant at the supposed neglect and inappreciation of his merit by the Royal Academy, he very early in his career placed himself in open hostility with that body, and has so continued till the present time. Of considerable talents, and with many good, social, and personal qualities, he has, by his overweening estimate of his own powers,

Jackson, and Collins. The Village Politicians measures about three feet by two, and is too well known to need description. The subject of Sunday Morning was the washing and preparation of a cottager's children for attendance at church. It was a small upright picture, about thirty inches high by twenty in breadth, and, in the general opinion, rather deficient both in the interest of the scene and the vigour of its execution. It was determined, on due deliberation, to send one only to the exhibition, and for this purpose some few voices were in favour of Sunday Morning; but the Village Politicians was ultimately decided on for that purpose, though Flaxman, who, as might naturally be supposed from the classical and antique refinement of his taste, had but little relish for rude nature, strong character, and rustic humour, held out small hopes of success from the experiment, advising the adoption of a totally different line of art for the neophyte's pursuit.

During the progress of the pictures, Mr. Stodart, while

and a passion for notoriety, run an eccentric course, of little advantage to any one, unless as a warning beacon. His life has been a constant succession of vicissitudes, which his indomitable pride and spirit have borne him through; and he is still struggling on (1839), with a numerous family, in the congenial but precarious occupation of an itinerant lecturer on the Fine Arts.

John Jackson. This admirable portrait-painter is an instance of the power of native disposition for a pursuit, in overcoming what might be thought insurmountable difficulties. He had worked as a tailor at Whitby, in Yorkshire, and was afterwards patronized by Lord Mulgrave. He earned a large income; kept a carriage, and lived beyond his means; was twice married, and died in the prime of life (1830) insolvent.

William Collins, son of a picture-dealer. His landscapes display great truth, freshness, and beauty, but, finding his popularity waning, he resolved to pass two years in Italy, from whence he is recently returned.

attending at Lord Mansfield's on his own business, mentioned
his young relation in terms of such warm recommendation that
his lordship called on Wilkie, and was pleased to engage the
Village Politicians for his collection, at the price of fifteen
guineas. But an event now occurred that put the painter in a
painful dilemma. The picture had been also seen by another
person who was willing to become its purchaser at thirty
guineas, and the artist could not but feel deeply, in his then
circumstances, the sacrifice of the larger sum. He resolved,
after some consideration, to make known to Lord Mansfield the
offer that had been made, and some discussion ensued, in which
his lordship required an acknowledgment of his right to the
possession of the picture, on the terms already agreed upon.
This Wilkie had never disputed, and, of course, did not hesitate
to accede to, when his lordship immediately told him that he
had always intended to give him thirty guineas, and that sum
was finally paid.

It may be readily imagined that, notwithstanding the most
rigid economy, Wilkie's resources at this time were inadequate
to his current expenses, small as those expenses might be. To
meet these he painted on small panels, or canvass, two or three
Village Politicians, and Blind Fiddlers, which he disposed
of through the medium of the shopkeepers who deal in the fine
arts. He applied, with this view, before he was at all known
in London, to different dealers in succession; among others to
Collins, of Great Portland Street, and to old Colnaghi, in
Cockspur Street; unsuccessfully to both, for the former said he
bought no modern works but those of George Morland, and the
latter, that the specimens shewn were not in his line of business.
Brydone, the frame-maker of Charing Cross, sold two or three
of these curiosities, one of them, a Blind Fiddler, for ten

guineas, to Daniel Stuart, of Brompton Park, editor of the *Courier*. Among his pictures not exhibited in London were two of some importance as to dimension, being each about three feet by two, the Village Recruit, and the Pinch of Snuff, as it has been very ingeniously named by its recent possessor. The former has been engraved, and the latter one has been recently (1839) purchased by the Baroness Rothschild, it is said, for nine hundred guineas.

When the exhibition at Somerset House opened in May, 1806, and the Village Politicians was seen by the public, Wilkie's reputation was at once established; the effect was electrical, and it might be compared without exaggeration to that produced by Lord Byron's Childe Harold. It was well placed, though not centrically, in the great room, and was from the first day constantly surrounded by a group of gratified spectators. Though not very forcible in effect, its simplicity of arrangement, its powerful expression, the novelty of its style, and beauty of its execution, excited an interest quite unexampled within the walls of the Royal Academy. He had been personally introduced by Jackson to Lord Mulgrave and Sir George Beaumont, and received commissions from each; and his next production was The Blind Fiddler, now in the National Gallery, for which he received fifty guineas, the sum agreed on in his engagement. Sir George very handsomely pressed double the amount upon the painter's acceptance, but the latter steadily refused it, and the baronet then insisted upon being allowed to fix his own price upon another commission then given (a small portrait of a gamekeeper, a favourite old servant), for which Sir George gave Wilkie a hundred guineas. The Blind Fiddler was painted in Soll's Row, Hampstead Road, where Wilkie had now removed, occupying a two pair of stairs floor in a very small house. In this admirable picture the figure, which gives it its title, was faithfully studied from a mendicant, well-known in London, where his most usual station was in Oxford Street, at the wall beyond Lord Harewood's house in Hanover Square. His fiddling was better than that of the generality of itinerant musicians.

Wilkie, whose principles of art being founded on truth and nature, never painted without a model, availed himself occasionally of the services of his friends, several of whom contributed in this way to the variety of characters displayed in his works; while his own plastic features, studied in the mirror, assisted his unrivalled power of expression on the canvass. The figure standing at the table in Village Politicians is a likeness, much overcharged, of himself; and portraits of his early companions, Callander, Stewart, and Macdonald, may also be traced in the groups of that picture, and in those of The Blind Fiddler. Both these extraordinary works were produced before the artist had attained the age of twenty-three.

About this period he painted two small pictures for a monthly publication of selected tales and essays; the subject of the one, The Clubbists, from Goldsmith, was very humorous, (engraved by Anker Smith for the book.) It afterwards became the property of Mr. Cattley, of Barnet; the other, The New Coat, from a tale of Voltaire, also published in the work, belonged to Mr. Stodart, of Golden Square. They were subsequently (1832) both engraved the size of the originals. While living in Soll's Row he painted for Mr. Alexander Davison. Alfred in the Neatherd's Cottage, and The Jew's Harp, for Mr. Annesley. A plate from The Jew's Harp, very cleverly engraved by Burnet, in the style of Le Bas's French prints, from Teniers, was published by Colnaghi in 1809, and was the first of Wilkie's engraved subjects that came before the public, with the exception of the two book-plates above-mentioned. The Alfred was engraved several years afterwards by Mitchell, but the picture had never been a favourite, the figure of the King, in particular, being generally considered not sufficiently dignified, either for the illustrious monarch himself, or for the purely historical character of the subject. It was a good deal larger than any that Wilkie had hitherto painted, more than double the size of the Blind Fiddler, and contained a portrait of the artist, a very correct likeness, in the background, in the costume of a huntsman, with a feather in his cap. Three hundred guineas was the price Mr. Davison paid for it. At his death it went into other hands, and is now (1839) in the possession of Hodgson and Graves, of Pall Mall. The Jew's Harp, on the death of Mr. Annesley, in 1813, was sold by auction, and being the first picture of Wilkie's that had ever been brought to the hammer, some interest was excited as to the marketable value of the commodity. It was knocked down to the Marquis of Blandford for seventy-eight guineas ; thirty was its original price, and the size about twelve inches by nine.

From Soll's Row he removed to a very comfortable lodging in Great Portland Street, Cavendish Square, and here he was attacked with an illness, the symptoms of which were at one time so formidable as greatly to alarm his friends for the ultimate consequences. He had the constant and most friendly attention of Dr. Baillie, and other eminent medical men, while the watchful solicitude of his noble patrons provided every assistance that could be of service ; but, above all, the affectionate care of his younger brother, Thomas, then settled in a mercantile house in London, mainly contributed to enable him to

struggle through the malady. When convalescent, he was
kindly invited to pass some time at Miss Joanna Baillie's
residence at Hampstead, for the benefit of change of air ; and
gradually, though slowly, recovered. He afterwards found it
necessary to regulate his diet and exercise with more than
usual circumspection.

This serious indisposition caused, of course, a great interruption in the progress of his labours, but he had previously
completed The Rent Day for Lord Mulgrave ; while The
Card Players, for the Duke of Gloucester, and The Cut
Finger, for Mr. Whitbread, were well advanced. Advised
to try a different air, he resided for a short time at Manor
Place, King's Road, Chelsea, and in 1811 he removed to Phil-
limore Place, Kensington, where his health became slowly but
perfectly re-established. He had received a commission for a
picture from Mr. Angerstein, through the agency of Mr. Lawrence (Sir Thomas), without limitation as to price, or stipulation as to subject. The exquisite picture of The Village
Festival, now in the National Gallery, was the result of this
engagement, and occupied his chief attention for nearly two
years. It has been said that the price charged for it was disputed ; this, however, is a mistake. When Wilkie named the
sum (seven hundred guineas), an expression of surprise at the
amount was certainly manifested by Mr. Angerstein, but no
dispute, or even delay, took place in the payment, and no interruption ensued of the friendly feeling of the patron towards the
artist.

For The Rent Day, one of his most celebrated productions,
he received one hundred and fifty guineas ; it is rather larger
than The Blind Fiddler, replete with character, and contains
many portraits. The centre group was painted from a sister

of Lady Mulgrave's, Mrs. Welsh, and the little girl from a daughter who died very young. The farmer standing at the head of the table is from old Tiffin, a well-known model of that time ; and the young man urging his suit on the unwilling steward, is an admirable portrait of Sam Strouger, one of the porters at Somerset House. The Card Players (a hundred and twenty guineas), after remaining twenty-seven years in Gloucester House, was sold by the Duchess, in 1839, to Mr. Bredell, the wine-merchant, for six hundred guineas. The Cut Finger, a small picture (forty guineas) is still in the possession of the Whitbread family.

In the year 1810 Wilkie was elected an Associate of the Royal Academy, attaining, in 1812, the higher grade of Academician ; and while his accession to their numbers reflected the highest honour upon the establishment, his successive labours have contributed largely to the productiveness of the annual exhibition. Without any intention of entering upon the *quæstio vexata* of the advantages or disadvantages attendant upon the institution of academies of art, it may be permitted to observe, that since the establishment of the Royal Academy in 1768, scarcely any names can be added to those lasting glories of English art, Hogarth, Sir Joshua Reynolds, Wilson, and Gainsborough, not one of whom had received an academic training, while hundreds of academicians, created during a period of more than seventy years, have passed like the shades of Banquo's progeny, leaving no recollections, and " making no sign." " How are they blotted from the things that be !" Wilkie is no exception, for, though on his arrival in London he became, for a short time, a student of the academy, and was claimed as a pupil (half in jest) by Fuseli, his most valued and peculiar powers were certainly formed long before, and in a very

different school—that of nature itself; the tendency of academies of art seeming rather to produce an indefinite number
of aspirants of mediocrity of talent than to inspire and foster
original genius.

Having resolved to hazard the experiment of a collective display of his works, taking the chances of profit and loss entirely
upon himself, Wilkie engaged a room in Pall Mall for this
purpose, and in April, 1812, his exhibition was opened to the
public; previous to which, a day was set apart, as is usual in
such cases, for a private view to his friends and patrons.
This might be said in more than one sense of the word to have
been nobly attended. Among the assembled visiters were the
Duke of Gloucester, the Marquis and Marchioness of Stafford,
Earls Grey, Mansfield, Mulgrave, Lord Kinnaird, Lady Holland, &c.; with baronets, knights, and esquires, too numerous
to detail; while the 'οι πολλοι was made up of artists, editors,
booksellers, together with the private friends of the painter.
It was remarked that only two or three members of the academy
were present; but whether their absence was merely fortuitous,
or was caused by a feeling of dissatisfaction at the circumstance
of a young man only twenty-seven years of age, and recently
elected one of their corps, presuming to call the public attention
to himself, independent of their establishment, was not ascertained. The following is a copy of the catalogue:—

A Catalogue of the Pictures, painted by D. Wilkie, R. A. now exhibiting
at No. 87, Pall-Mall. Admittance, one shilling. Catalogues gratis. London: printed by C. H. Reynell, 21, Piccadilly. 1812.

The Public are respectfully informed, that (permission having been
granted by the proprietor to Mr. Wilkie); an engraving will be made by
Mr. Raimbach, from the original picture of VILLAGE POLITICIANS. The
size of the engraving will be twenty-two by sixteen inches, being the same

as that of the print of the *Blind Fiddler.* The price to subscribers will be two guineas—proofs, four guineas: half to be paid at the time of subscribing, and the remainder on delivery of the print.—The best impressions will be strictly appropriated to the earliest subscribers.

Subscriptions will be received at the *Exhibition Room,* No. 87, *Pall-Mall;* at Mr. Wilkie's, *Kensington;* and at Mr. Raimbach's, No. 10, *Warren-Street, Fitzroy-Square.*

CATALOGUE.

Those that have been exhibited at the Royal Academy are marked thus*.

No. 1. The New Coat, from the tale of Jeannot and Collin —*Voltaire,* . . . 1807.
2.* Village Politicians . 1806.
3.* A Gamekeeper . . 1811.
4. Blindman's-Buff(unfinished)
5. Jew's-Harp . . . 1808.
6.* Blind Fiddler . . 1806.
7.* The Cut Finger . . 1809.
8. The Sick Lady. . . 1808.
9. The Village Holiday. 1811.

In the principal group of this picture, a man is represented hesitating whether to go home with his wife or remain with his companions at the public-house.

" On ae hand, drinks deadly poison
Bare ilk firm resolve awa';
On the ither, Jean's condition,
Rave his very heart in twa."
                              Macneil.

10. A Family Picture . 1810.
11. Portraits of a Clergyman and his Wife . . . 1807.
12.* The Rent-Day . . 1807.

13. Portrait of a Lady of Quality . . . . . . 1807.
14. Alfred reprimanded by the Neatherd's Wife for his Inattention to the Toasting of her Cakes . . . * . . 1806.
15.* The Wardrobe Ransacked . . . . . . 1810.
16.* The Card Players . . 1808.
17. The Sunday Morning . 1805.
18. Sketch of The Blind Fiddler.
19. ——— of The Village Politicians.
20. ——— of The Wardrobe Ransacked.
21. ——— of The Sick Lady.
22. The Country Fair (1.) 1804.
23. Sketch of the Jew's Harp.
24. ——— of The Rent Day.
25. ——— of Boys digging for Rats, (2.) 1811
26. ——— of Alfred in the Neatherd's Cottage.
27. ——— of The Card Players.
28. ——— of the Cut Finger.
29. Study from Nature, of a Gipsy Woman and Child, 1810.

* History of England.
                              M

1. This is one of the artist's earliest pictures: most of the figures in it are portraits of the inhabitants of a small village in Scotland, where the fair is annually held, and near to which the picture was painted.

2. The picture of which this is a sketch was painted last year, and is placed in the Council-room of the Royal Academy, as a diploma picture.

FINIS.

The picture of Blind-man's Buff was painted on a commission from the Prince Regent, and remains in the royal collection. The Sick Lady, the size of the Blind Fiddler, was purchased by the Marquis of Lansdowne, for a hundred and twenty guineas; and after his death, the Marchioness disposed of it, and at length it came into the possession of Mr. Moon, the printseller, who published in 1839 an engraving from it by Engleheart, under the title of The only Daughter. A Family Picture, containing the portraits of Mr. and Mrs. Nield and their children, was about twenty-four inches by eighteen, and a hundred guineas was paid for it. The portraits of the Clergyman and his Wife were the worthy parents of the artist—that of the Lady of Quality was the Dowager Lady Mulgrave; both small pictures. The Wardrobe Ransacked, an upright picture, about eighteen inches by twelve, remains in Lord de Dunstanville's family. The Country Fair, about four feet by three, was painted at the age of twenty, and though, as might be expected, very imperfect in execution, and all the mechanism of the art, contains evident indications of Wilkie's peculiar genius in several humorous groups, some of which served him afterwards as detached subjects of more finished character. The sketches were all small, differing both in size and degree of completeness from each other. This exhibition of his works no doubt contributed to extend the already established celebrity of the painter; and during the three months of its remaining open, was visited by nearly twenty thousand persons. Its actual profits, greatly diminished by various contingencies, were very small.

With health re-established, he now proceeded with and completed the Blind-man's Buff, and commenced the Distraining for Rent. The former was bought for the Prince Regent, at the price of five hundred guineas; the latter remaining for several months without a purchaser, though the sum asked for it (six hundred guineas) was admitted on all hands to have been moderate. An offer was made from Mr. Hart Davies, of Bristol, but declined by Wilkie; the terms of payment somewhat resembling those of the priest in the old story—*moitié en messe, moitié en argent*. The proposition was, that Wilkie should receive, as part of the price, a valuable picture from Mr. Hart Davies's collection, but of which some doubts as to its originality were candidly stated by that gentleman, and the residue in money. Distraining for Rent has been generally acknowledged to be one of Wilkie's most admirable works. Its simple, pathetic, and clearly-told story; its truth and variety of character; its force and beauty of expression; its solemnity of effect; and its excellence of drawing, colour, and execution, place it altogether in the very first class of his productions. The objection was to the subject; as too sadly real, in one point of consideration, and as being liable to a political interpretation in others. Some persons, it is said, spoke of it as a "*factious* subject." The British Institution, to its honour, bought the picture solely on its merits, thereby fulfilling one of the most important functions of their establishment as a society for the promotion and encouragement of native art. During the uncertainty as to its sale, and when Wilkie expected the picture would remain on his hands, he still expressed great satisfaction at having made the experiment, and thereby proved that he was not to be estimated merely as a painter of *comic* scenes, a designation under which the public seemed disposed to consider him, but which he felt, with the modest and becoming confidence that was inherent in his nature, was doing him less than justice.

Several years afterwards, when party-spirit had perhaps somewhat subsided, the Directors were prevailed on, with some difficulty, to sell the picture at its original price, for the purpose of engraving, to Mr. Raimbach, of whom Mr. Wells, of Redleaf, its present possessor, purchased it in the year 1830 for eight hundred guineas. Some change in Wilkie's domestic arrangements was caused by the death of his father, which took place in 1813, and which led to his mother and sister coming from Scotland and residing with him, to the great comfort and satisfaction of all parties. Mrs. Wilkie was one of that invaluable race of women, that may still be occasionally met with, though not often, in these latter times of forced and superficial systems of female education. The gentle and affectionate temper and disposition of the mother, combined with the intelligent and active though quiet exercise of a perfect knowledge of household management as the mistress of a family, rendered Wilkie's domestic life a model of " man's best delight, well-order'd home ;" while the manners and accomplishments of his sister, Miss Wilkie, a worthy daughter of her parentage, contributed a degree of elegance and refinement, that graced his establishment suitably to the station of such a man.

At the restoration of peace and the Bourbons in 1814, Wilkie, accompanied by his friend Haydon, made an excursion of a few weeks to Paris, embarking at Brighton at the latter end of May for Dieppe, and passing through Rouen. This,

his first visit to a foreign country, was replete with interest to Wilkie, and the impression made on his mind by the total change of scene which presents itself in so striking a manner to travellers on landing at Dieppe, gave him a most agreeable foretaste of the enjoyment in store. According to his own statement, the pleasurable effect of the novelty and contrast of all that now met his eye, with the objects hitherto familiar to him, was scarcely equalled, certainly never exceeded, afterwards in the prosecution of his journey. Without being a proficient in the language, he had sufficient knowledge of French to be able to make himself understood, and to understand tolerably well its ordinary and accustomed phraseology, though his natural diffidence induced him most frequently to depend on the more confident agency of his fellow-traveller's interpretation. Soon after his arrival, the fatigue of his journey, combined with the excitement of the various wonders of art, not then restored to their original owners, concentrated in Paris, brought on an indisposition that induced him to seek medical advice. Happily, either with the assistance of the doctor, or in spite of it, he soon recovered, and was enabled fully to enjoy and profit by the unlimited access to the various collections and establishments so liberally afforded by the French, and so peculiarly gratifying and advantageous to artists. He visited many of the eminent painters, and met, of course, with the usual kind and urbane treatment that so pointedly distinguish their reception of strangers.

Among the incidental occurrences of this excursion, Wilkie's proceedings with the French printsellers should not be forgotten, as strikingly illustrative of the modest and unassuming perseverance belonging to his character. He had taken with him a few impressions of the Village Politicians, then recently published, with the view of introducing the engraving to the knowledge of the Parisians, and his method of proceeding was to sally out in a morning with a roll of the prints under his arm, and call at the shops of the different dealers, submitting his merchandize to their inspection. As might be expected, he met with but small encouragement in his pains-taking efforts from these patrons of the art on this occasion, (strongly contrasting with subsequent success,) while his own candour and conscious superiority were displayed in his frank and humorous relation of the circumstances attending each unsuccessful application. The printsellers, not aware of the quality of their applicant, generally admitted that the engraving was not without some merit, but that the subject was utterly unsuited to the refined and classical taste of the French nation, and was evidently only calculated for the *Low* Countries (*Les Pays Bas.*) They all, to a man, declined to venture the smallest speculation in the *article*, though offered on terms that might have tempted them on ordinary occasions. These negotiations ended, *re infectâ*, by some impressions being left on sale or return with a M. Delpech, when Wilkie came back to England. Before he quitted Paris, however, he had the satisfaction to hear that one had been sold ; the purchaser was the leader of the band at one of the theatres, the *Odéon*. The sale of the Wilkie prints in France has since become very extensive. After a most agreeable sojourn, Wilkie returned home in July, leaving Mr. Haydon in Paris.

In this year's (1814) exhibition at Somerset House appeared the two subjects of Duncan Gray and The Letter of Introduction, both admirable pictures, and intended respectively for Dr. Baillie and Mr. Dobree. The Letter of Introduction was the popular favourite, and from this circumstance

Wilkie learned a lesson, which he afterwards generally adhered to, namely, not to exhibit companion pictures the same year, thereby avoiding the inevitable comparison between the two, which must be injurious to one or the other. In the present case, The Letter of Introduction proved the most popular, and Mrs. Baillie, wife of the Doctor, wrote to Wilkie, expressing her hopes that it was destined to ornament her drawing-room. Wilkie, in this dilemma, could only regret that the arrangement suggested was impossible, Mr. Dobree's portrait being introduced in the favourite picture at that gentleman's desire. After the exhibition, the pictures were sent to their respective proprietors, and Duncan Gray was received at Dr. Baillie's with avowed satisfaction. But Wilkie was not a man to rest satisfied in such circumstances. He quietly proceeded with another subject of the same size, The Pedlar, which, when completed, he sent to Mrs. Baillie, requesting that, if preferred, it should be retained instead of Duncan Gray. This handsome conduct was abundantly acknowledged, and Duncan Gray returned to the painter, with whom it remained a rejected picture till purchased some years afterwards for its original price (a hundred and fifty guineas), by Lord Charles Townshend, and was knocked down at Christie's, in 1835, at the sale of Lord Charles' collection, for five hundred guineas, to Mr. Sheepshanks, and still forms (1842) one of the chief ornaments of that gentleman's exquisite assemblage of modern pictures.

In 1816, Wilkie made a short tour in the Netherlands, and, returning by Calais, he encountered a similar adventure to that of Hogarth in the same place, as indicated by our great moral painter in his print of " O ! The Roast Beef of Old England." While in the act of sketching the gate, he was interrupted by

an officer of police, and *invited*, as the French phrase is, to
attend with him before the Mayor of the town. After a brief
explanation of the circumstances, it was intimated to Wilkie
by that functionary that no drawings were allowed to be made
from any part of the fortifications. He was dismissed with
civility, and permitted to retain his unfinished sketch. The
observation was made in England that Wilkie, from a wish to
re-enact the Hogarth drama, had put himself in the situation
expressly that he might be arrested ; but nothing could be further from the general tenor of his conduct, distinguished as it
had always been by unobtrusive manners and simple, unaffected
modesty ; and, in the present case, most assuredly the remark
had no foundation whatever.[3]

[3] " On travelling through France, the most singular occurrence was that
of my being arrested at Calais, in the act of completing a sketch of the
celebrated gate of Hogarth. A young Englishman, who had come from
Lille with me, had agreed to remain with me while I was making the
drawing; and as I had first obtained leave from the officer of the guard, I
expected no sort of interruption. After I had been at work, however, about
an hour, with a great crowd about me, a *gendarme* came to me, and with
an imperious tone said : ' *Par quelle autorite faites vous cela, monsieur ?*' I pointed to the officer on guard, and told him that he had given
me leave. ' *Ce n'est rien—c'est défendu, monsieur. Il faut que vous
preniez votre livre et m'accompagniez à l'Hôtel de Ville.*' This, of
course, I agreed to most willingly, and beckoning my friend to go too,
I went along with him, with all the people staring at us. At the Hôtel de
Ville we were requested to go to the mayor, and as we were marching
along to his house the *gendarme* said, '*Voila le maire—arrêtons.*' We
stopped till the mayor came up, and learning from us what was the matter,
he dismissed the *gendarme*, took us back to his house, and told me, that as
there were a number of people there, as in other places, who, on seeing a
foreigner making a drawing of a fortified place, would naturally suppose it
to be from a hostile intention, and finding it done *en plein jour*, would

When Wilkie had completed his picture of Blind-man's Buff, for the Prince Regent, he received a commission from his Royal Highness to paint a companion to it. The Penny Wedding, now also in the royal collection, was the subject chosen by the artist, and when finished was submitted to the Regent's inspection at Kensington Palace, on occasion of his Royal Highness's visit to that residence in the course of an examination of the various pictures belonging to the crown. The fine taste and sound judgment possessed by the Prince in matters of art have been generally acknowledged, and, indeed, the splendid show of Sir Joshua Reynolds's finest whole-length por-

be apt to blame the magistrates for allowing it, he said it was necessary, therefore, that I should not go on with my drawing, although, from examining it, he was satisfied that I only did it for amusement, and, therefore, regretted the interruption."

The above *naive* account of the arrest is from one of Sir David Wilkie's letters to my father. The remaining part refers chiefly to matters of business, but a few sentences gathered from it will furnish a brief account of his tour in Holland and return home.

" I left Antwerp the second day after you were gone, about noon; got to Breda that night, and next morning made a most agreeable journey by Gorcum and Utrecht, and reached Amsterdam late in the evening. From Amsterdam I went to Harlem to breakfast, by the canal, and heard the celebrated organ, which was really wonderful, and certainly finer than the one at Ghent. I dined at Leyden, which I reached also by the canal, and at night got to the Hague. I was induced to stop a day here. The day after I went to Rotterdam; and the day after that, making altogether eight days, I returned to Antwerp. I expected to hear something of Haydon when I got to Brussels, but finding that he was not come, and that the weather was quite broken up, I gave up all intention of again visiting the field of Waterloo. I, therefore, resolved to make the best of my way to England by the way of Calais."

The date of the letter is October 8, 1816, and the earlier part of the tour is narrated in the preceding memoir.—M. T. S. R.

traits that adorned the great dining-room at Carlton House, collected by his Royal Highness, formed no common evidence of this reputation being well founded. Some of these noble pictures were unfortunately destroyed, and others of them greatly damaged, by an accidental fire, which, for a time, threatened the destruction of the entire building. This irreparable loss included that surpassing *chef-d'œuvre* of Sir Joshua, the portrait of the Duke of Orléans, the father of the present King of the French. The liking of the Prince for the art led naturally to his notice of the artists themselves, and Hoppner, Lawrence, and Wilkie, had all of them personal experience of the generous disposition, kindness, and affability, so peculiarly belonging to his character.

In the year 1822, on the occasion of his Majesty's memorable visit to Scotland, Wilkie took advantage of the opportunity of combining professional objects with the renewal of old friendships in his native country, and, in view of the former object, was to be seen in pretty close attendance on the movements of the Court. On his return, he commenced the picture of George the Fourth's reception by the nobles and people at Holyrood Palace. The execution of this fine composition remained a long while suspended, from various causes, and was not completed till 1830. It now forms part of the royal collection. In the mean time, Wilkie produced his admirable picture of Reading a Will, on a commission from the King of Bavaria ; and, among other works, the finished sketch, as it is called, of John Knox preaching to the Lords of the Congregation, afterwards purchased by the Earl of Egremont, on terms that did honour to the well-known liberality of that venerable nobleman. Reading a Will was greatly admired by George IV., who expressed a wish to possess it. A sort of

negotiation ensued, through the medium of Sir Thomas Lawrence, the Bavarian Envoy, and Wilkie, which ended very properly in the final destination of the picture to Münich, where it
now makes part of one of the most magnificent galleries of art
in existence. The pre-arranged sum paid to the artist was
four hundred guineas. This affair afforded Sir Thomas Lawrence the opportunity of paying a very courtly compliment to
Wilkie, on the circumstance of Kings striving for the possession of his works, which was not badly replied to by him, that
to Sir Thomas belonged the still greater honour of arbitrating
between the contending monarchs.

The health of Wilkie's excellent mother had been declining
for some considerable time, but without any appearances to
excite more than the usual anxiety attending a gradual decay,
when symptoms highly alarming suddenly supervened. Mrs.
Wilkie's sufferings were soothed by the most affectionate and
unremitting watchfulness of her amiable and accomplished
daughter, the frequent presence of her younger son, Mr.
Thomas Wilkie, and with the indulged hope of again seeing
the justly considered pride of her heart, David, who happened
at the moment to be absent in the North. But, alas! it was
not to be. He had been written to immediately on the change
appearing, urgently pressing his instant return ; and, though he
made every possible effort, he did not reach home until a few
hours after the fatal event. Mrs. Wilkie died, and was buried
at Kensington. Her funeral was attended by her two sons,
David and Thomas, Sir James M‘Grigor, Dr. Darling, Mr.
Mushet, Mr. Stodart, Mr. Young, Mr. Raimbach, &c.

The shock of his mother's death occurring under such painful
circumstances had a most distressing effect upon Wilkie's health.
A slow, consuming malady fell upon his nerves, and after a time

rendered him quite incapable of practising his art. The highest surgical and medical skill was, of course, available to him, but the science of the most eminent practitioners was at fault, and Wilkie's case, like most others of the class called nervous disorder, baffled their utmost resources. Cheltenham, and other such places celebrated for their health-restoring reputation, were tried in succession, but without the smallest benefit to the patient, and finally the doctors recommended (as is usual with them in all similar cases) a long course of travel, and a total abstinence from all attempt at professional occupation. In pursuance of this advice, Wilkie, in autumn, 1825, left England for the continent, accompanied by his relation, Mr. David Lister, a young student in the medical schools of Edinburgh. The first point of destination was Paris, where he arrived in so very precarious a state that some of his friends, whom he met with, became exceedingly alarmed, and, doubtless with the best and kindest intentions, contributed to aggravate rather than alleviate his malady by various contradictory medical opinions. One of the most startling annunciations, and made to the patient himself, was, that his disease was neither more nor less than an *amollissement du cerveau,* the Esculapius urging, at the same time, the prudence of an immediate return, by easy stages, to the bosom of his family. Happily, Wilkie's natural discernment and firmness of mind enabled him to estimate, at their just value, the opposing oracles of the faculty, and, though perplexed in the extreme by his officious advisers, determined to act upon his own judgment, to discard the doctors, and continue his travels.

At this period the star of Wilkie seemed to be no longer in the ascendant ; its brightness was doomed to undergo a temporary eclipse, but it was only for a time, as it happily re-ap-

peared, and with added lustre, on his return to England, in
restored health, in 1828, after an absence of more than three
years, passed in Italy, Spain, and Switzerland.   The Royal
Academy exhibition was deprived of its most valuable support,
and the public showed that they missed their favourite painter.
He had regularly contributed to the exhibition at Somerset
House, some of its chief attractions; among them may epeci-
cially be noted the Reading the Gazette of Waterloo, which
was so surrounded by the crowd of spectators, that Wilkie
determined, after the first day of its opening, to have a barrier
rail erected for the purpose of guarding it from casual damage.
It is scarcely too much to say, that the benefit accruing to the
Academy funds from the exhibition of this picture may be
estimated at not less than a thousand pounds.   During the
progress of this great work, for which he received twelve hundred pounds in bank-notes from the hand of the Duke himself,
at Apsley House, and the same amount for the copyright of
the print, from Messrs. Moon, Boys, and Graves, Wilkie had
painted several small pictures, one of them, Smugglers Alarmed,
for Sir Robert Peel ; the subject suggested by the recent occurrence, of the capture and trial of a band of notorious freebooters.
Sir Robert introduced and accompanied the artist to Newgate,
in furtherance of his study from nature and truth ; the basis of
his art, and his invariable practice.   The last picture he exhibited before he left England (1825) was an exquisite specimen
of his talent, A Highland Family, painted for the Earl of
Essex ; and he had made some admirable studies and sketches
for pictures which, alas ! have never been completed ; particularly one of A School, and one of The Arrival of a Rich
Relation.

To return to Wilkie in Paris. He remained in private apart-

ments, tolerably comfortable for French lodgings, assiduously
attended by his young friend, David Lister, and visited, as he
improved in health, by Sir Thomas Lawrence (who was then
employed painting the portraits of Charles X. and the Duke
of Angoulême, for George IV.), Mr. Alfred Chalon, and several other of his English, with some French friends; until,
after some weeks' residence, he found himself strong in body,
as he had long been determined in mind, to extend his journey
to the south. In consequence, at the beginning of October, he
made a very prudent and judicious written bargain with a
voiturier, and set out at an early hour in the morning for
Switzerland. He bore the journey much better than could
have been expected, considering his reduced and feeble state.

Wilkie reached Geneva without mishap, but with enough of
incident among his fellow-travellers to counterbalance the
ordinary monotony of the journey, and of which he gave a very
agreeable narrative in one of his letters.[4] He had borne the
fatigues of the journey very well, travelling by easy stages in a
roomy though somewhat clumsy vehicle, and resting occasionally at night at certain stations on the road.

The soothing and judicious attentions he experienced in
Geneva, from his friend Mr. Topfer, and, through that gentleman's introduction, from many of his connexions of the highest
respectability, produced the happiest result. His health gradually though slowly amended, but it was yet a long while
before he attempted to resume his professional occupations.
Still, however, while unable perhaps to engage in the actual
practice of his art, he was constantly storing his mind with
novel and additional materials of great value, which was abund-

[4] See Appendix.

antly manifested in the pictures of Italian, Spanish, and Swiss subjects, exhibited after his return to England.

Having discarded his doctors, he found himself so much stronger that, after a discreet lapse of time, he felt sufficiently recovered to venture to dispense with the companionship of his young friend Lister, who returned to Scotland to pursue his medical studies, leaving Wilkie, when they arrived at Milan, to continue his journey to Rome and Naples by himself; and the event fully justified this determination, no ill consequence whatever ensuing from it.

It was not in England alone that Wilkie's fame as an artist stood high. His celebrity might truly be termed European ; and as no man could be better entitled to distinction, so neither were honours ever borne with more unassuming modesty and diffidence. It has been said that great and acknowledged talents can afford to be modest. Doubtless they may, but they are, nevertheless, too seldom found so disposed. In Wilkie the feeling, if it ever existed in man, was genuine and unaffected, forming, as it were, a part of his very nature ; for though, of course, well aware of and perfectly competent to estimate his own powers, he was habitually as free from arrogance of manner, or the assumption of any thing like superiority, as he was above the mean and contemptible vanity, which cloaks but not conceals itself under a pretended and exaggerated humility.

In every city in which he occasionally resided on the continent,—in Paris, Rome, Naples, Florence, Madrid, Geneva, München, &c.,—he met with the most gratifying reception, from distinguished individuals, both of his own and of foreign countries. At Rome, in particular, a splendid entertainment, presided at by the Duke of Hamilton, was given in honour of him, a grand account of which, with the speeches made on the occasion, appeared afterwards in the *Times* newspaper.

He returned to England in 1828, with renewed health and spirits, though his personal appearance did not at first quite re-assure his friends, being pallid and reduced, to which no doubt the fatigue of his journey home had partly contributed. His natural diffidence also led him to feel great anxiety as to the reception that the pictures he had brought with him might meet with ; more especially as their style of execution differed materially from his former productions. This change had not arisen either from choice or caprice, but originated almost wholly in the necessity, occasioned by his illness, of his adopting a less elaborate mode of execution than that of his earlier works. A very short time, however, sufficed to remove all uneasiness upon this subject from his mind, and he quickly regained both strength and cheerfulness. His Spanish subjects were submitted to the inspection of the King (George IV.), and were most graciously approved ; the painter himself receiving distinguished marks of his Majesty's kindness and liberality at the same time. These pictures now make part of the royal collection, and this period may be noted as the commencement of the King's marked patronage of Wilkie, that continued unabated to the end of his reign. Several of the Italian subjects became the property of Sir Willoughby Gordon, and add greatly to the value and interest of that gentleman's very choice collection of Wilkie's works. Sir Willoughby possesses, among the number, the small whole-length portrait of the Duke of York, which, as a work of art has, perhaps, never been surpassed by any master, ancient or modern.

The liberal patronage of George IV. was further manifested by his Majesty in sitting to Wilkie for his portrait, a whole-

length, in Scottish costume ; and on the death of Sir Thomas
Lawrence, by his appointment to the place of Principal Painter
in Ordinary. The duties of this office consist in painting and
superintending the sovereign's portraits for state presents to
foreign countries, embassies, &c. ; for all which the artist is
duly paid, in addition to the annual stipend of £200. Wilkie
also at this time executed many commissions for portraits of
individuals, greatly to their satisfaction in most cases, and
equally to his own advantage and professional credit, notwithstanding a good deal of invidious criticism, which of course,
under the circumstances, was naturally to be expected.

It was confidently anticipated by the public, or rather that
small section of the public that takes any interest in such matters, that the presidency of the Royal Academy—the highest
accredited station of the fine arts in this country—would, on
the death of Sir Thomas Lawrence, have naturally devolved on
Wilkie. As the acknowledged head of the English school, his
claims were recognized by all Europe, and favoured by his own
monarch, but were set aside by the election of Mr. Shee.[5] The
general feeling of surprise on this event was neatly hit off in
the often-quoted epigram—

> See Painting crowns her sister Poesy!
> The World is all astonished !—so is *Shee.*

At the time of Wilkie's return from abroad, the numerous

[5] This highly accomplished gentleman is not less amiable in manners
than distinguished by varied talents. Poetry and oratory can each claim
in Sir Martin a favoured votary. His *Rhymes on Art* are not mere imitations of the versification of Pope, but ingenious and animated satires,
replete with taste, truth, vigour, and good sense. His prompt and fluent
speeches at the Royal Academy meetings are no less celebrated.

N

publications, known by the name of Annuals, were in the ple-
nitude of their fashionable popularity. Short-lived as it was
doomed to be, the success was so great, that their proprietors
were enabled to offer unheard-of sums for the privilege of engraving from the selected works of some of our favourite painters.
Wilkie was too valuable a prize to be allowed to escape the
importunities of these speculators ; and, tempted by the pecuniary advantages so seasonably administered, he was induced
to accede in a few instances to their propositions ; but, soon
perceiving the tendency of these works to bring art and artists
to the same dull, dead level, he at once resolved on declining
all further contribution of his pictures to them.

Fortune was now again smiling upon Wilkie. The doubts
and apprehensions of a renewal of the public opinion in his favour (which only his unassuming diffidence in the strength of
the talent he displayed could have given rise to) were soon
dispelled. The marked personal notice he received from George
the Fourth, together with the truly princely remuneration of
his Majesty's various commissions, followed as these were by
others from the greatest and noblest in the land, opened a career to our painter equally splendid, lucrative, and flattering.

On the accession to the throne of William the Fourth, Wilkie
was continued in the office of Principal Painter to his Majesty,
and executed, as part of its duties, some whole-length portraits
of the king, and also of the queen Adelaide. He subsequently
painted several of the Duke of Wellington, the Earls of Mel-
ville, Montague, &c., and found that the preparation of pictures of such dimensions was attended with much inconvenience
in a house of small apartments. He therefore had to make up
his mind to one of two evils—either to a change of residence, or
the building of rooms suitable to his purpose. With charac-

teristic caution, he took ample time for consideration, and
finally decided on choosing the former, as the least annoying
of the alternatives. A handsome and spacious mansion, called
the Vicarage House, in Kensington, becoming vacant, he determined on taking possession, finding it equally eligible for a
domestic establishment and for his professional occupations. It
was also a fitting home for the "foremost man of all the world"
in his department of art, a proper place of reception for his numerous distinguished visiters, and was situated in a locality
(Kensington) to which he had acquired, during a residence of
twenty-five years, an habitual attachment.

It was in June, 1836, and during the Whig administration,
that Wilkie received the distinction of knighthood from the
hands of William the Fourth. It was more especially the
affair of Lord John Russell; and it has been a matter of some
wonder that the Tories should have thus suffered their political
opponents to gather this honour for their party, of performing
an act of obvious justice; particularly as Sir Robert Peel was
the artist's personal friend, as well as one of his greatest
admirers, and a most liberal purchaser of his pictures. The
ceremony took place at a *levée*, in the ordinary way, and was
attended also in the ordinary way by some good humoured jest
of his Majesty on the Christian name of David, (for the "gentle
monarch ever loved a joke") and as to the certainty of its not
being Saul! On retiring back to the crowded circle, Wilkie
felt the eager pressure of a friendly hand on his, and, turning
his head, found it proceeded from Lord John Russell, who
warmly congratulated him on his newly-won dignity — so well
merited, and so judiciously conferred.

On the decease of William the Fourth, Wilkie became the
chief painter to Queen Victoria, being the third sovereign in

succession to whom his services had been devoted. In addition
to the usual state portraits, he was commissioned to paint Her
Majesty's First Council, for the royal collection : a subject
interesting from the number of portraits it contained of illlus-
trious and distinguished personages, who were officially brought
together on that occasion.

Among the larger works he now produced was that of the
discovery of the body of Tippoo Sultaun, after the storming of
Seringapatam by Sir David Baird. The high encomium that
has been so justly bestowed on Goldsmith — *nihil tetigit quod
non ornavit*—may with equal truth be applied to Wilkie, as
this very successful picture goes far to prove, being of a description of subject as far removed as can be conceived from his
usual course of study and habits of thought. The truth and
nature, the character and expression, displayed with such admirable life and energy in The Village Politicians, The Blind
Fiddler, and The Rent Day, the first works exhibited, by their
unrivalled superiority so completely identified Wilkie as the
painter of a peculiar class, that, on each successive deviation
from his original track, he had not only to undergo the severest
of ordeals in a comparison with himself, but also to encounter
the natural unwillingness in the human mind, even of the most
candid, to acknowledge a plurality of excellence in the same
individual ; not to mention the inevitable accompaniment,
more or less skilfully disguised, of professional envy and de-
traction. All this has been abundantly manifested in regard
to Wilkie's labours in portrait, history, and landscape, in all
which he has produced pictures of first-rate ability, sufficient of
themselves to establish a high reputation for their author in
each several department, independently of those works peculiar
to himself, and of such universal celebrity as to have given his

name to a class, as " Wilkie pictures." It may be unnecessary to cite a large number of his works to justify this opinion ;
one of each department will be sufficient: in history, the picture of John Knox preaching to the Congregation in Scotland ;
in portraiture, that of H.R.H. the Duke of Sussex ; in landscape, the Sheep-washing, in Sir Thomas Baring's collection,
will all equally well establish Wilkie's transcendent talent and
versatility.

It is given to but a very small proportion of competitors in
the difficult pursuit of the fine arts to attain to a high degree of eminence ; and exertions not less arduous are necessary to maintain an elevated station, than to "climb the steep
where Fame's proud temple shines afar." There is no standing
still. *Non progredi est regredi.* No man could possibly show
himself more sensible to this emphatic truth than did Wilkie.
As long as his health permitted, he never slackened in his
efforts to enlarge his knowledge and improve his practice ;
while, to support an artist's popularity, he considered it indispensable to introduce from time to time a change in the nature
and choice of his subjects. With these views, he omitted no
favourable opportunity of visiting other countries, that might
afford him materials for scenes that would by their novelty and
variety excite an additional interest in the public. In 1835 he
went to Ireland, and the result was the admirable picture of
The White Boy's Cabin, which he doubtless intended to follow
with other Irish subjects, as occasions might be afforded consistently with his various engagements, when, in evil hour, he
was prompted to undertake that fatal journey which ended in
his premature death !

The extensive tour he had projected — to countries offering to his observation and study a field both rich and novel,

including the cities of Constantinople, Jerusalem, and Alexandria — was commenced in the autumn of 1840 ; and he was accompanied by Mr. William Woodburn, the eminent picture-dealer, with whom Wilkie had previously travelled in Spain. His brother and sister, Mr. Thomas Wilkie and Miss Wilkie, were in constant correspondence with him, and received letters from him with tolerable regularity. His usual health, never robust, had suffered some interruptions, caused probably by the change of climate, but not so material as to excite alarm. He had been away about ten months, had laboured incessantly, (sufficiently shewn in more than two hundred sketches and pictures), and had certainly overtasked his strength, when, prompted perhaps by some internal warnings, he determined at once to return home. He accordingly embarked at Alexandria, leaving Cairo unvisited, in the Oriental steam-vessel, on the 23rd May. He arrived at Malta on the 27th, from whence he wrote in cheerful spirits to his sister, apprising his friends of his progress, and the near approach of their meeting, and that his health was at that time better than it had been. At Alexandria, the quarantine officer, in the customary official report on the state of health of the passengers, described Wilkie as of about sixty years of age, of rather enfeebled appearance, as if from over-fatigue, but without any positive malady, &c. This description answers well to a man brought by excessive exertions to a certain degree of debility, and to a look of more years than he actually numbered. On the 31st of May, the Oriental reached Gibraltar, and, having sent the letters on shore, pursued her homeward course. The company were assembled in the saloon, and Wilkie had not yet been seen. His fellow-traveller, Mr. Woodburn, went to seek him, and found him still in bed. He inquired if he was disposed to join the party at breakfast, and Wilkie expressed such to be his intention. Not however making his appearance, after the lapse of a considerable interval, Woodburn naturally felt alarmed, and hastened again to Wilkie's cabin, and was shocked to find him unable to speak coherently and nearly insensible. There happened to be several medical men, passengers, on board, and their assistance was instantly in requisition. But, alas! all human aid was unavailing; and this truly great artist and good man yielded to the common lot, under circumstances of more than usual distressing interest. The captain of the vessel, at the request of the passengers, put about and returned to Gibraltar, with the view of obtaining permission to land the body. The application was made, but without success, the Governor being unable, in any case, to dispense with a rigid observance of the quarantine laws. Had it been within the power of the authorities to have relaxed the severity of the rule, there can be little doubt that it would have been exercised in the instance of so eminent a name as that of Sir David Wilkie: as it was, however, the vessel directed her course to England, and, as she quitted the Bay, the remains of this distinguished man were committed to the deep, amidst the regret of all on board, and with such solemnities as the nature of their unprepared situation enabled them to bestow. The proximate cause of death, according to the opinions of the medical men, was serous apoplexy, brought on by over-exertion, excitement, and anxiety. Thus, alas! prematurely ended the career of Wilkie, leaving a name that takes its place by right among the most illustrious of British Artists, and embalmed in the hearts of his sorrowing relations for his affectionate and generous disposition; while his memory will be long cherished by numerous friends, for the perfect integrity, candour, and modesty, and for the unaffected simplicity of manners by which he was characterized.

Sir David Wilkie in person was above the middle height, well-proportioned, and of spare habit. His features were marked by the national (Scottish) peculiarities, and were prepossessing and placid in their ordinary expression : when animated by discussion, they became strongly lighted with fervour and intelligence. His conversation was perfectly unassuming, and replete with shrewdness and good sense. His constitution was delicate, and he had suffered some severe attacks of illness ; one of long duration in 1825, which seemed completely to baffle medical skill, and led by advice of the physicians to his lengthened visit to the Continent. Notwithstanding these serious checks, his temperate and careful habits and prudent conduct were sufficient to warrant the hope of his life being extended yet a good many years, on the principle that with due care a vessel of porcelain may last as long as an iron one ; when he was induced to make his last voyage, contrary to the opinions and advice of some of his friends. A three-quarters portrait by Phillips and a bust by Joseph represent him at two different periods, and are considered good resemblances. In the Exhibition of 1842, were two pictures by Turner and Jones, founded upon the melancholy ceremony of his funeral at sea.

In April, 1842, the sale of his pictures and sketches took place at Christie and Manson's, and excited a degree of public interest quite unprecedented. The sale continued seven days, and produced about nine thousand pounds—nearly double the amount that was anticipated. This sum, added to about twenty thousand pounds he had previously realised, was bequeathed chiefly to his brother and sister, the only survivors of the five children of his father's family. Wilkie's habits of life were moderate and unexpensive; and while his generosity to his brothers and family was extensive, the economy and excellent management of his mother and sister co-operated with his own constant care and prudence, to make that reserve from his income that secured his independence in any case.

The death of this great artist under such melancholy circumstances excited a universal feeling of regret; and the general sympathy was manifested, not merely by a barren and momentary expression of sorrow, but in the immediate adoption of measures for raising a permanent tribute to his memory, in a marble statue, to be placed in the National Gallery. Meetings were held at which Sir Robert Peel presided, and which were attended by Lord John Russell, the Duke of Sutherland, Lord Mahon, Sir Charles Forbes, Sir James M'Grigor, Sir Peter Laurie, the Poet Rogers, and a numerous assemblage of members of Parliament, gentlemen, artists, and others, all prepared to do honour to the distinguished man whose loss they deplored. A subscription was commenced; and at the first public meeting, at the Thatched House Tavern, about £1000 were subscribed, (subsequently increased to £1700) and which, after some discussion in the Committee of Management as to the appropriation of a small part of it, for the establishment of a Wilkie medal for an annual prize to the Students in Painting, was finally allotted to the monument alone.

An exhibition of his pictures to the number of a hundred and thirty took place at the British Institution, Pall Mall, in 1842, which continued open during June, July, and August, and two small whole-lengths of the Sultan and Mehemet Ali were in the Royal Academy exhibition.

APPENDIX.

Rome, Poste Restante,
January 10, 1826.

My dear Mr. Raimbach,

After parting from you, where you so obligingly met us in our starting from Paris, we proceeded day after day with the vetturino, jogging on slowly towards the south-east frontier, a journey monotonous, but not without adventures. A quarrel took place between two Frenchmen one night at supper with us, which next morning after we started cost one of them his life. On the eleventh day we descended in the Canton de Vaud, in presence of the Alps, and entered Geneva. Here meeting my friend Topfer, introductions and hospitality were not wanting, and we passed four days most agreeably in true native Genevese society. The good Audeoud alone I was not permitted to see; a violent fever had lately attacked his weak and mutilated frame, and, though better, he could see no one, and those acquainted with him forbade even the leaving a card, as a thing too exciting for him.

We parted for Lausanne and Vevay, proceeded up the Vallais, and crossed by that wonder of wonders, the route of Mount Simplon, whence in a short space we found ourselves in the gay and classical

scenes of Italy, with all the associations of its former greatness, and
present interesting decay before us.   Art being my object, as it would
be yours, the Last Supper of Leonardo da Vinci drew my attention
at Milan.   Time, however, with this has been even more unsparing
than is his wont.   A shadow only remains of this once great work,
and that so faint, that even the substance of the original paint has
become a question whether fresco, tempora, or oil : but to show the
immortality of *mind*, when such a thing is to be found in a picture,
over the frail *material* with which it is embodied, this masterpiece, in
its very ruin, has been revived in the admirable engraving of Morghen, and seems yet destined to enjoy a wide posthumous existence
long after the walls of the Dominican refectory have crumbled
into dust.

From Milan, by Pavia, we passed to Genoa, a splendid city without,
but loathsome within, where a few, and but a few, pictures rewarded
the search ; thence by the coast of the Mediterranean, along the tops
of the Apennines to Pisa, where the Falling Tower and the Campo
Santo court attention, the latter presenting upon its walls a series of
the early efforts, before painting reached its maturity, evincing at
once the lowness of its infancy with the high and spiritual aim which
even from that it attained in its growth.   From this we passed to
Leghorn, and thence to Florence.

Here Phillips and Hilton soon joined me from Venice ; and our
conjoint researches from gallery to palazzo, and from chiesa to convent, among the early, the matured, and the later masters, found full
occupation for a month.   One object with me here, though defeated,
was to see and converse with the venerable Raphael Morghen.   His
bottegha, for such his studio partly is, is a resort of many travellers,
who buy at first-hand impressions of his works, which, numerous and
exhausted as the plates must be, he still sells in tolerable though grey
condition, and, besides this continuing source of wealth, is said to be
a man of considerable substance.   From Florence our next resting-
place was to be the Imperial City itself ; six days by vetturino was to

bring us in sight.   We chose the unfrequented road through Sienna,
celebrated for the purest Tuscan, as Lochaber is for the purest Gaelic
— I suppose from its inaccessibility to strangers.   Here, through
wildness, desolation, and volcanic sterility, over barren hills and fetid
valleys, the climate cold and wintry, reversing all that Claude has
painted or that poets have described, we drove along, and, at last,
passing the extended and swelling but pestilential *campagna*, we
entered Rome, where, putting up, fatigued as we were, we hurried
over intricate streets and muddy Tiber, and before twilight found
ourselves in the expansive interior of St. Peter's, where even the
most extravagant of our expectations were realized.   I felt now
that after my fatigues, after all the sorrow and sickness with
which I have been afflicted, a great event was accomplished, I was
now in Rome, and one of the brightest dreams of my youth come
to pass.

The labours of Michael Angelo and Raphael have since been the
chief object of my study, by far the most intellectual.   They make
other works appear limited, and, though high in all that is great,
are still an example, and a noble example too, of how the accessaries
of a work may be treated with most advantage.   No style can be so
pure as to be above learning from them, nor so low and humble as
not to gain even in its own way by their contemplation.   They have
that without which the Venus and the Apollo would lose their value,
and with which the mean forms of Ostade and Rembrandt become
instructive and sublime, namely, expression and sentiment.   To some
of the younger artists here, however, I find they are a stumbling-
block; things to be admired but not imitated, and less to be copied
than any flat, empty piece of Venetian colouring that comes in their
way.   The effect of these works upon the unlearned public at large
deserves attention.   Fresco, when old, gets dull and dry, and cannot
be repaired or refreshed like oil; their impression therefore upon the
common eye is not striking; and many people acknowledge this who,
show them a new print from Raphael or Michael Angelo, would be

delighted. Vividness is perhaps necessary to make any work generally impressive ; and suppose these fresh as they were at first, and
as I have seen some recent frescoes, I believe they would be the most
beautiful things imaginable — popular beyond a doubt, as it is on
record they were so.

In modern art Rome is the school for all other countries, though
opposite styles are here to be found suited to each. In painting, the
Italians and French are alike followers of David. The English students, excepting Lane, whose picture has not yet been seen by human
eye, are chiefly occupied with subjects of Roman costumes; but the
Germans, for devotedness, more like a sect than a school, have
attracted much attention by their novel experiment of copying the
masters and precursors of Raphael, not Raphael himself, in hopes
that passing over the same course they will arrive at his excellence.
They have also revived the art of fresco, which, as they manage it
better than they do oil, proves it at least as easy; and, though their
system scarcely admits of originality, it yet has so much of expression,
and discards so much of what is meritricious, that I wish their feeling
were infused a little into ourselves. Their names are Schnorr, Veit,
Schadow, and Overbeck. Schnorr takes the lead, has married a
Catholic, and changed his religion to feel more devoutly the scriptural
subjects of his art.

But it is sculpture here that is the great object of attention and
encouragement. The numbers of these artists multiply by every
day's further knowledge of Rome. The chisel and mallet are heard in
every corner. Amidst such competition, great talents have and are
still rising. True it is, that seeing at all hands statues and groups
arising, with almost faultless form and in pure Greek taste, one's
notions of the difficulty of imitating the antique, and even one's
respect for the antique itself, are somewhat diminished. But knowledge of the figure and correct form will not of itself make high art.
Canova had much more than this, or he never would have impressed
as he has done. He added grace and intelligence ; and, although his

taste, adored as it was, is passing away, and Thorwaldsen, with more severity, more style, but with less expression, has risen in his place, a blank is still left. Draperies prevail over flesh, and flesh over feature; and sculpture will, like painting, become mere decoration, if the expression of the inward man does not occupy some share of its attention.

With objects passing around one, with all the antique remains and local associations of this enduring place, you may believe time does not hang heavy. The English society, too, is so numerous, and, at such a distance from England, lay so completely aside their national reserve, that as a stranger I never felt more at home; and, having full leisure, and no immediate care or anxiety, and with strength, and even the appearance of health, and most excellent spirits, I may say the present is a time of most satisfactory enjoyment. Yet still I have not much to boast of. Time is left to do every thing with my complaint. I have given up medicine, and would almost give up the doctors too for any good they can do. Still I am not worse than I was when I left you in Paris.

My sister has informed me you had been to Kensington after your return from France; and she stated, much to my satisfaction, your having been to visit the Baron Gérard at Auteuil with our worthy president. I wished you should see the baron, assured as I was you would be well received. I think such a party must have been gratifying to you. As we are now old friends, may I state a suggestion upon this, namely, considering that it is not every artist that is so qualified for general society as you are, should you not in London go more into society than you do? Some people feel this as a duty to their profession—it would relieve, not hurt your studies. This is taking a liberty with you, but it arises from my respect for qualities to which I look up more than any other feeling; and rest in mental is as necessary as in bodily occupations.[1]

---

[1] This kind urgency produced no effect. To a singularly retentive memory, an acquaintance with general literature such as is seldom met with, and an

And now, my dear sir, give my kindest regards to Mrs. Raimbach and to all the young people, not forgetting little David. They will recollect, I doubt not, our meeting in the Louvre. And as, at such a distance, one likes to hear of one's friends and what they are doing, may I ask you to favour me with a letter to tell all the news — how the published plate goes on, how you proceed with your more serious labours, and what you think can be done next to carry on the war?

Yours very truly
DAVID WILKIE.

To Abraham Raimbach, Esq.

THOMAS UWINS, ESQ. TO A. RAIMBACH, ESQ.

Naples, April 11, 1826.

My dear Raimbach,

It is not want of inclination, nor want of thinking of you, that has prevented my writing, but the fear that I could not make a letter sufficiently interesting to authorize its being conveyed to such a distance. I have written to nobody since leaving England, besides my own family, except Williams, Joseph and Alfred Chalon, with all whom I have been placed in circumstances to render writing a matter of business and duty; and it is more a feeling of duty than any other

inexhaustible fund of anecdotes, told with inimitable humour and effect, as must be well remembered by the few friends with whom he was in the habit of familiar intercourse, my father united a reserve and shyness, fostered by the solitary nature of his profession, that made him shrink from all contact with strangers. —M. T. S. R.

(I freely confess it) that induces me now to make this attack on your friendship and patience.

I once made a negative sort of complaint of Wilkie's behaviour to me when we met in the *gude toon* of Edinburgh. If I had any reason at that time for complaint, which is a doubtful matter, he has given me abundant occasion lately for feelings of a different character. It would be difficult to explain to you to what extent his friendly attentions have been useful and beneficial to me; and they came in a way, too, that was flattering to my vanity, always the most pleasant side on which to attack a man. He seemed to seek me out as something to repose on — as a shelter from the common-places of the lounging travelling gentlemen, by whom at every stage it was his fate to be surrounded. He came and sat with me in my study, freely criticised my works, suggested improvements, explained to me much of the arcanum of the art with which I was unacquainted, and even went so far as to work on one of my pictures. In this last effort I encouraged him, not merely for the good it was doing me, but from a sincere hope that, finding the palette and brushes again in his hand, he might get the confidence to do something for himself, which confidence, could it be inspired, would do much towards restoring him to health—luckily he asked for nothing that I had not got ready to his hand. The moment he named a colour, it was upon the palette with the rapidity of lightning. I knew if anything was wanting it would be an excuse, in his state of nerves, for stopping altogether. All my exertions, however, would not do; in a few minutes he threw down the palette and brushes, and made me take up what he had abandoned: it seemed as if feeling himself at work again so unexpectedly had a different effect on his mind from what I hoped. He either was, or was determined to think himself, incapable of the requisite exertions. I did not attempt to push the thing, but rather got rid of it entirely by proposing a walk to the palace (a gentleman's house is always a palazzo here), where some of my works are hanging on the walls. My good friend Sir Richard Acton happened to

o

be at home, so I introduced him at once to my patron and my pictures.

We afterwards made two excursions together—one of three days' journeying to Pæstum, taking Pompeii and the Museum at Portici in our way; and the other to the crater of Vesuvius. I acted as interpreter, but not as bargain-maker. Wilkie and his cousin soon took my stewardship from me: they beat me out and out in negotiating with the Italians.

Wilkie wrote a letter in the Temple of Neptune at Pæstum, the extreme point of his travels, another in the ruins of Pompeii, and a third on the summit of Vesuvius. This is a touch of the *art de se faire valoir* that is quite beyond me; or rather I am not great man enough to make a letter any more interesting from rocks and stones than it would be from my own writing-desk in my own humble study. People may say what they will about the modesty of genius, but I never yet saw great talent unaccompanied with a sufficient portion of confidence; and that timidity which has prevented my putting myself forward in the world is really the effect of conscious weakness. This very consciousness has stood in the way of my writing to you and to other friends. My brothers I know are interested about me, and I can torment them with my *longueurs* without any fear of tiring their patience or offending their taste; but it is not easy to task myself into the opinion that any body else will have the same charity for me. It is having Wilkie to talk about that has made me bold; and now I am in for it I will give you the other page of myself.

I have really got good by coming to Italy, and still more by coming to Naples. I have been thrown on my own resources. I have practised the art here alone, and I have proved to myself what I never did know before — the extent of my powers. If I were ten years younger I should reap more benefit from it; but, old as I am, I cannot think of it without thankfulness and gratitude. To tell you all that has passed through my mind on examining the works of the great heroes of the great ages of art would go beyond the measure of my sheet. But I must venture to say that they certainly thought less about fine drawing and academic accuracy than as students we are led to believe. Raphael and Michael Angelo are full of inaccuracies, and abound in violations of all the precepts of the schools; and Correggio is anything but a fine draughtsman. The style of thinking in the two first is what we must most admire, and the last is a fine example of style in painting. No one can enter the Vatican and Sistine Chapel without having his conceptions of the powers of art elevated. He seems to be holding commerce with beings of a superior order; to be treading on new ground, and expatiating in a world which, though it may before have formed the matter of his waking dreams, has never before been brought round him in so tangible a shape, or so connected with *his own business and his own bosom*. I do not mean to argue from this that we ought to avoid the study of what is fine in form or accurate in delineation; but I think the object and end of art ought to be set more before students than it is. But I must not talk of these matters till I have been at Bologna. All the world seems captivated with that city; and the great authority in criticism, Mr. Hazlitt, told me in Rome: "Sir, I patronize *Guido*." Whatever he saw at Bologna I know not, but I am sure he saw *nothing* at Rome, or saw what is to be seen so hastily and imperfectly, that whatever he writes on the subject must be mere invention.

I believe I am a bit of a truant from all the schools, for, to tell you the honest truth, I have spent quite as much time in the open air, amidst rocks, and woods, and precipices, or in cottages, amongst the simple inhabitants of the mountains, as I have in churches and picture-galleries. Nature keeps the noblest school, after all. Her lessons never tire—line upon line, and precept upon precept; and the more we have the more we thirst after. None can tell but those who have come to the same feast with the same feelings the excessive enjoyment I have had in these glorious scenes; it is a rich country

for people of all tastes.   The scholar wanders about with his Virgil
and Horace, the geologist with his chisel and hammer, and the
botanist with his tin case, and all return satisfied ; but no one that I
have heard tell of it has spoken of its romantic character.   In this
light it has made more impression on my imagination than even the
splendid scenery of the Alps ; and under this aspect, if I live to get
home, I shall endeavour to represent it.   There are scenes, too, with
which the elegance of high life so exactly assimilates, that I have
sometimes fancied myself back in the days of Boccaccio—and this is
not difficult.

   The fascinating Countess of Blessington has been living at the
Villa Gallo, a place which contains within itself every beauty that
the most poetical imagination can desire ; and when you add to this
the charms of its enchanting occupant, and the class of people by whom
she is surrounded, what can be wanting to make Boccaccio's scene
complete ?   I have found myself one of a party, dining on a beautiful
grass-plot near the house, where caverns in a dry rock formed the
most romantic chambers ; trees gave us a delicious shade, and birds
warbling supplied us music ; the good-humoured hilarity of the noble
hostess, the archness of her pretty sister, the elegance of the accomplished Count D'Orsay, and the unceasing fun of Sir William Gell,
made up the rest of the entertainment.   Sometimes Fox, the eldest
son of Lord Holland, a young man of extraordinary talents, formed
one of the group, and won the hearts of all by his singular story-
telling powers — a talent he possesses in a higher degree even than
Walter Scott.   Old Mathias, too, the once renowned author of the
Pursuits of Literature, fills up a niche in the style of the old school
with his poetic allusions and classic quotations.   These are a few of
the characters who were to be seen at the Villa Gallo ; but, alas ! the
enchantress is gone, and the magic circle drawn round her is broken
and destroyed !   Florence now possesses her, and the scene of her
influence is transferred from the bay of Naples to the banks of the
Arno.

I should tell you that the little picture to which Wilkie did me the honour to put his hand has since been bought by Woodburn; this I have a right to consider a great point of distinction and patronage, and the more so, as it is the only thing he has bought here. He has been friendly enough to take it to the ambassador's, where it is seen by all the English of rank who visit Naples. I am delighted to have to record an instance of friendly feeling in a picture-dealer towards a living artist.

Yours ever and most sincerely,
THOMAS UWINS.

For Abraham Raimbach, Esq.

THOMAS UWINS, ESQ. TO A. RAIMBACH, ESQ.

Palazzo Campana, Vico Belle Donne,
Naples, January 9, 1827.

My dear Raimbach,

Sitting down to acknowledge the receipt of your valuable and beautiful present brings to my mind so many sins of neglect and procrastination, so many resolutions made and broken, and so much left undone that ought to have been done, that I am deprived of half the pleasure arising from communication with a loved and valued friend, by the self-reproach that accompanies the act and hangs about my spirits in the performance of it. I have now been three years exiled from my country and my friends, but I can assure you the strong attachment to those few in whose recollection my name has been allowed to retain a place is rather increased than diminished by absence—and in proportion to the distance which separates us is the intensity of the feeling that carries me back, from time to time, to their homes and their firesides, and mixes me up with their interests and occupations. Never shall I forget the first sight of your beautiful engraving of Blind-man's Buff. Independently of my admiration for it as a work of art, there is an interest about every inch of the subject, whether background or figure, chairs turned upside down, or boys tumbled over head and heels, things however important or however trifling, all bring to my mind some conversation I have enjoyed with you, or some hour I have spent in your study, while your hand was engaged in driving along the unpromising tool by which these magic wonders were achieved.—Poor Wilkie! his late visit to this place has made the charm of your united labours complete. It is delightful to find the characters of men who do great things always in accordance with their works.

Believe me, though I seem to linger here, and though these luxurious scenes and this delicious climate all invite my stay, yet there is a voice within that whispers Home and England. You will have heard from my brothers that I have been rambling over the north of Italy since I last wrote to you, studying all the great schools of art on the ground where they flourished, and revelling in the intellectual feast which this glorious country still offers to all who have appetite and taste. It is humiliating to find that a very few names give the character to each school, the rest have sunk in merited obscurity. Whatever men may be in their own eyes in their own days—however they may have been puffed up with self-importance, and strutted and fretted in the midst of their cotemporaries, Posterity knows them not—their works are passed over like the tapestry hangings of a room—the eye does not rest upon them, nor does the mind acknowledge them. It is truly wonderful to see how soon the influence of bad taste enters. A school is scarcely formed, the lives of its founders have scarce expired, before it begins to degenerate; and the tide of bad taste once set in, nothing can stop it—it goes on " *di male in peggio*," till whole ages are occupied in multiplying insignificance and giving birth to

nothingness. There is one period of art only that has a decided intellectual character. It is that which preceded what is called the revival.
Giotto and Cimabue, with a host of others of the same age, have left,
scattered through the churches and convents of Italy, such thoughts
as would be sufficient to inoculate any country with good taste, provided they were fairly published and circulated. Were I a young man
instead of an old one, I would seriously set about careful outlines of
the selected works of this age, as the foundation on which my future
exertions might be wisely based. It was in this school even more
than in the antique that Flaxman studied, and it is following soundings
left by Flaxman, that the Germans are now making such discoveries
and such progress, as will lead to the regeneration of taste throughout
Europe. You do not know, however, how to honour Flaxman in the
country of his birth. England should set up a monument to his memory
in every important town from north to south; children should be taught
to lisp his name, and a relish for his works should be infused into the
instructions of the nursery. Lawrence will be recollected long after
his death—Wilkie may wear out some ages—but Flaxman will live
for ever.

It is the fashion with the English to spend this part of the winter
in Naples; and here they are, shivering in rooms without fireplaces,
and exposing themselves to the pitiless pelting of storms, from which
neither cloak nor umbrella can screen them. This winter as well as
the last, and I suppose all the winters of Naples, are enough to bother
the invalids who come for a mild and equable climate. We have all
the varieties of weather in the course of one day! and such winds!
and such hail! and such rain! every street presents an impassable
torrent, and it is one of the offices of the *lazzaroni* to let out their shoulders to those who are able to pay for being carried over. But all
this, bad as it is, suits me better than the damp atmosphere of
England. The rain, it is true, does come down in torrents; the
thunder does roll its terrible fury over our heads, and seldom passes
without striking some fated victims; earthquakes not unfrequently

make us tremble in our beds; but when all is over (and it does pass over quickly) the sun shines out again with a charm irresistible, the air is filled with refreshing sweetness, and so little remains of the dreadful agitation, we are inclined to doubt the accuracy of our recollections.

I walked out lately towards the sea, my usual morning custom. The terrific roaring of the winds and waves had disturbed me throughout the night, but in the morning all was peace. The sun shone gloriously, and the face of nature presented an aspect of smiling serenity. Not all, however, were to rejoice that morning in the sun's cheering rays. A boat had been wrecked in the bay, and the shore was literally strewed with dead. Two men and a woman were thrown close under the wall of the Villa Reale; one man had his faithful dog locked in his arms; the rest of the bodies, fourteen in number, became visible as the agitation of the sea subsided: three persons only reached Naples alive. The day before this, the son of a military officer at the Ponte Maddelena was struck dead by lightning close to his father's side. These things happen constantly, but they make little impression. The only newspaper published here is not permitted to report the circumstances, so that they are little known beyond the immediate neighbourhood of the disaster, and there but partially and imperfectly. Death has presented itself lately in another shape. A party of our own wise compatriots, determined to be above the prejudices of the country, had been shooting for ten days in the Pontine Marshes. Returned to Naples, they were ashamed to tell they were ill, till fairly laid on their beds with *malaria* fever. All have suffered severely, and one, Mr. Scott, of a noble Irish family, is dead.

All sorts of titled and distinguished folks have found their way here this winter, though the list at Almack's I suppose will hardly be sensible of the diminution. The Prince Leopold complains the English newspapers worry him to death, and force him to seek on the continent that independence of opinion and action denied him in his foster country. The member for Durham and his lady wife are striking the

Neapolitans dumb with a display of riches and magnificence hitherto
unknown on the shores of the Mediteranean. Here are Marquesses,
Countesses, Bishops, Baronets, and ladies with every variety of titled
and untitled opulence. One man, a Mr. Turner, has left a good
estate and a comfortable fireside, and is wandering over the world
for no other purpose than to persuade every body to swallow white
mustard-seed. A table-spoonful taken three times a-day is to cure
all disorders, and to prolong life to a period much beyond the average
of former generations. Possessing so important a secret, this benevolent old gentleman would consider himself criminal if he allowed
his fellow-creatures to remain ignorant of its virtue. Another man
(a Mr. Empson, of Oxford University, in holy orders) has no object
in removing from place to place but *la Pasta*. He followed this
celebrated *cantatrice* from London to Paris, and from Paris to Naples.
The time of his stay in a place is regulated by her engagements with
the stage-managers. Do not mistake—it is not love—he is not personally known to her — it is simple admiration of her astonishing
powers. Whenever she sings, Mr. Empson is stationed in the pit,
at an angle in which no look, no action of his idol can escape his eye.
Till the opera concludes he remains immoveable, and then goes home
quiet and satisfied to bed. Another man, educated for the Scottish
church, has been to Constantinople, and returns filled with the doctrines and fascinated by the followers of Mahomet. If he preaches
at all, he is determined to make the Koran his text-book.

Naples is rich at this moment in dreamers and enthusiasts, and the
king on the throne is amongst the most distinguished of the class.
Money has been left by some devout personage to buy golden crowns
for the ten Madonnas in the Neapolitan dominions who have the reputation of working the greatest number of miracles. The claims of
the different wooden or painted deities have been discussed with due
solemnity by the Pope and the Cardinals; and a small four-feet
image in the church of *Jesu Vecchia* has obtained the prize for this
city. The crown was placed on the head of the little Queen of

Heaven by the Archbishop of Naples, the king and royal family following the procession with wax-candles in their hands.   The church
was crowded to suffocation to witness this, as the newspapers call it,
"sublime spectacle;" and, ridiculous as it may appear to you, it is
only a very small part of the mummeries and abominations daily
practised by the Romish priests to cheat and deceive an ignorant and
superstitious people.   Popes, kings, courts, and ministers of state
are the only parties that do not grow wiser as the world grows
older.

Pompeii is a point of perpetual and never-ceasing interest.   Olives
have been found in pickle so fresh as not to have lost their form.
New painting, and other works of ancient art, are daily unearthed,
and exposed to the gaze of the curious.   The pictures abound in
graceful combinations, whatever other qualities they may want, and
however various they may be in the charms of execution.   There
must have been a more general diffusion of taste among the ancients
than has ever been obtained in modern times.   Still let us not be
carried away with the prejudice that all they did was beautiful.
Things of the most disgusting character have been discovered in
public places, to say nothing of the decorations of the wine-shops,
and other houses devoted to immoral purposes: and even in taste
the ancients were not always right.   A fountain has lately been
exposed in a private garden not one whit more refined than similar
things in the gardens of White Conduit House or Bagnigge Wells,
to which, indeed, this remnant of antiquity bears a most striking
resemblance.

That my friends of the Dilletanti Society in London may not
accuse me of presumption in talking thus freely about works done
two thousand years ago, I propose making drawings of many things
hitherto passed over in silence; and, to satisfy the English Roman
Catholics on the subject of papistical superstition, it is my intention
to make a picture of one of those shops which abound here, wherein
are carved, painted, and sold crucifixes, madonnas, saints, angels, souls

in purgatory, and all other matters necessary to the public and private worship of the church of Rome.

" He burneth part thereof in the fire — and the residue thereof he maketh a god, even his graven image: He falleth down unto it, and worshippeth it." — ISAIAH, c. xliv. v. 16, 17.

Believe me, my dear Raimbach,

Yours ever faithfully,

THOS. UWINS.

To A. Raimbach, Esq.

THE END.

LONDON:
F. SHOBERL, JUN. 51, RUPERT STREET, HAYMARKET,
PRINTER TO H. R. H. PRINCE ALBERT.

www.ingramcontent.com/pod-product-compliance
Ingram Content Group UK Ltd.
Pitfield, Milton Keynes, MK11 3LW, UK
UKHW012347130625
459647UK00009B/589